EVERYTHING YOU NEED TO KNOW ABOUT THE VOICE

T0244578

MEGAN DAVIS is the Balnaves Chair in Constitutional Law, Director of the Indigenous Law Centre at UNSW Law and Pro Vice-Chancellor at UNSW. She is the leading constitutional lawyer on Indigenous constitutional recognition and was a member of the Prime Minister's Referendum Council, Expert Panel on Constitutional Recognition and the Referendum Working Group. She is a United Nations expert based in the UN Human Rights Council, Geneva and formerly UN New York. She is a Cobble Cobble woman from south-west Queensland.

GEORGE WILLIAMS AO is the Anthony Mason Professor and a Scientia Professor, as well as a Deputy Vice-Chancellor, at UNSW. He was a member of the Australian government's Constitutional Expert Group that advised on the wording of the Voice referendum. His books include *Australian Constitutional Law and Theory*, *The Oxford Companion to the High Court of Australia* and *How to Rule Your Own Country: The Weird and Wonderful World of Micronations*. He has appeared as a barrister in the High Court of Australia and is a columnist for *The Australian*.

MEGAN DAVIS &
GEORGE WILLIAMS

EVERYTHING YOU NEED TO KNOW ABOUT THE VOICE

UNSW PRESS

UNSW Press acknowledges the Bedegal people, the Traditional Owners of the unceded territory on which the Randwick and Kensington campuses of UNSW are situated, and recognises their continuing connection to Country and culture. We pay our respects to their Elders past and present.

A UNSW Press book

Published by
NewSouth Publishing
University of New South Wales Press Ltd
University of New South Wales
Sydney NSW 2052
AUSTRALIA
https://unsw.press/

A catalogue record for this book is available from the National Library of Australia

ISBN: 9781742238111 (paperback)
         9781742238814 (ebook)
         9781742239750 (ePDF)

Design Josephine Pajor-Markus
Cover design Jenna Lee
Cover image Uluru, taken on the eve of the consensus, the Uluru National Convention, 2017 (photograph by Jimmy Widders Hunt)

All reasonable efforts were taken to obtain permission to use copyright material reproduced in this book, but in some cases copyright could not be traced. The authors welcome information in this regard.

CONTENTS

INTRODUCTION

Australians will soon be faced with an important choice. Will they vote Yes to change our nation's Constitution to introduce an Aboriginal and Torres Strait Islander Voice? Or will they vote No and bring the recognition process to a halt and, along with it, the aspirations of an overwhelming number of Australia's first peoples? The stakes could not be higher.

The Voice referendum will be Australia's first attempt to amend the Constitution in nearly a quarter of a century. The last time a change was put to the people was in 1999, when they rejected the idea of a republic and a new preamble (or opening words) to the Constitution. We have to go back much further again to find the last time that Australians voted Yes to constitutional change. This was in 1977, nearly half a century ago.

This referendum matters because it is the culmination of decades of advocacy and public debate about how our nation can come to terms with its past, and prepare for a better future, by recognising Indigenous peoples in our nation's founding document. Changing our Constitution to bring a new body of Indigenous peoples to advise on the laws and policies that affect them offers the best – and only – opportunity to achieve this. The referendum promises to be a moment of national inclusion that will for the first time recognise our first peoples as part of the nation formed upon their ancestral lands.

This could mark a decisive break from the Constitution that came into force at Federation in 1901. That document excluded Indigenous people from the political settlement that brought about the new nation. Rather than being treated as equal citizens, they were cast as a 'dying race' not expected to survive British settlement. They were described as a 'problem' and as a people lacking any future in the nation. As a result, they were immediately denied the right to vote in federal elections and the Constitution said they could not be included in counts of the Australian population. As Australia celebrated its passage into nationhood in 1901, Aboriginal and Torres Strait Islander peoples were herded onto reserves and missions. These are two very different experiences of Federation.

This referendum and moment of nation-building is different. Australians will vote on change that embodies the aspirations of Aboriginal and Torres Strait Islander peoples for how they would like to be recognised in the Constitution. This was made clear at a historic gathering of Aboriginal and Torres Strait Islander peoples at Uluru in 2017. They issued a statement to the Australian people on what constitutional recognition should include. The Uluru Statement from the Heart (see pages 192–93) called for a First Nations 'Voice' to Parliament protected by the Constitution followed by a process of agreement-making and truth-telling. This is popularly referred to as Voice, Treaty, Truth.

This is not the first time that Australia's first peoples have sought constitutional change. Their advocacy culminated in a successful referendum in 1967. Since then, many people – including a long list of Aboriginal people and Torres Strait Islanders and successive prime ministers from Paul Keating and John Howard onwards – have agitated for further change. These calls emerged as it became clear that the 1967 referendum had left unfinished business.

The 1967 referendum deleted discriminatory references to Aboriginal people but put nothing in their place and provided no means for them to have a say on the laws and policies that affected them. As a result, rather than recognising Indigenous people and giving them a voice, the referendum left a silence at the heart of the Constitution. Today, the document reflects Australia's history of British settlement but fails to acknowledge the much longer occupation of the continent by Aboriginal and Torres Strait Islander peoples. It is as if this history does not matter and is not part of the nation's story.

The 1967 referendum also did not deal with other issues of importance to Indigenous peoples. These include the settlement of differences through the making of treaties and the need to have a say on laws that affect them. In bypassing these and other issues, the 1967 referendum failed to make structural changes to improve the relationship between the state and Indigenous peoples.

Some people find it hard to see why these issues should be tackled when so much else needs to be done. The evidence time and time again illustrates the disadvantage Aboriginal and Torres Strait Islander peoples experience and how this manifests in poor life expectancy and unemployment. One of the ways of addressing this is constitutional recognition.

Overcoming disadvantage requires multiple approaches.

An Indigenous Voice is one of the things that could accelerate improvement.

Constitutional change of this kind can have broad, positive effects that extend far beyond the law. For example, the referendum could unite Australians around a sense of their shared history which, for the first time in the Constitution, would include the long habitation of the continent by Aboriginal and Torres Strait Islander peoples. This is reflected in the fact that the Uluru Statement from the Heart was issued as an 'invitation' to the Australian people to work with First Nations peoples on a journey that would repeat what was done in unity in 1967. The invitation explained why constitutional change is so integral to improving the situation of Indigenous peoples in Australia.

Constitutional recognition could also have positive health effects. Research on the social determinants of health shows how legal discrimination and exclusion can have a negative impact on mental and physical wellbeing. Indeed, it is hard to underestimate the emotional and other costs of being cast as an outsider in your own land. Experts have recognised this. For example, the Royal Australian and New Zealand College of Psychiatrists notes:

> The lack of acknowledgement of a people's existence
> in a country's constitution has a major impact on their
> sense of identity and value within the community,
> and perpetuates discrimination and prejudice which
> further erodes the hope of Indigenous people. There
> is an association with socioeconomic disadvantage
> and subsequent higher rates of mental illness, physical
> illness and incarceration.

Recognition in the Constitution would have a positive effect on the self-esteem of Indigenous Australians and reinforce their pride in their culture and history. It would make a real difference to the lives of Indigenous Australians, and is an important step to support and improve the lives and mental health of Indigenous Australians.[1]

Examples from other countries (such as Canada, New Zealand and the United States) highlight how the right legal settings can produce better health outcomes. The hope is that changing the Australian Constitution to recognise and empower Aboriginal and Torres Strait Islander peoples will contribute in the same way.

Our goal in this book is to set out what people need to know to understand the Indigenous Voice and our nation's journey towards constitutional recognition. This means exploring where the Constitution came from, and the role Indigenous peoples played in its drafting.

We also examine how the Constitution was altered in 1967, and why that referendum has led to calls for further change today, including most prominently through the Uluru Statement and its call for the Voice.

This book is uniquely placed to tell this story. Megan Davis, the first author of this book, was a member of the Referendum Council and designed the regional dialogue method that led to the consensus at Uluru on 26 May 2017. She read the Uluru Statement from the Heart to the national convention and then the Australian public for the first time. Megan also advises the Australian government as a member of its Indigenous Referendum Working Group and as a member of its Constitutional Expert Group. She has examined constitutional change processes including citizen conventions and deliberative democracy and more importantly Indigenous constitutional change processes globally and has drawn upon the experience of those working with communities including Aunty Pat Anderson, Noel Pearson, Patrick Dodson, Dalassa Yorkston, Galarrwuy Yunupingu and many others who work and live in Aboriginal and Torres Strait Islander communities.

George Williams, the second author, has also been involved with many of the contemporary events described in this book in his work as a constitutional lawyer. As a barrister he appeared for the Ngarrindjeri women in the *Hindmarsh Island Bridge Case* in 1998 and has provided support and advice on matters including the making of treaties and constitutional recognition to parliaments and organisations such as land councils, the National Congress of Australia's First Peoples, ATSIC and the Council for Aboriginal Reconciliation. He also serves as a member of the Australian government's Constitutional Expert Group advising on the wording of the Voice referendum.

TIMELINE

Since time immemorial Aboriginal and Torres Strait Islander peoples have lived on the land now known as Australia for at least 60 000 years.

1770 Captain James Cook claims the land now known as Australia.

1788 Captain Arthur Phillip and the First Fleet arrive at Botany Bay.

1846 Exiled Tasmanian Aboriginal people on Flinders Island petition Queen Victoria about agreement made with Colonel Arthur.

1881 Petition from residents of Maloga Mission (Yorta Yorta) to NSW Governor seeking land grants (residents soon after moved to Cummergunja reserve).

1886 William Barak wrote from Coranderrk: 'We should be free like the White Population there is only few Blacks now rem[a]ining in Victoria … and we Blacks of Aboriginal Blood, wish to have now freedom for all our life time'.

1890s Debates over a federal Constitution: Aboriginal and Torres Strait Islander people not involved and barely mentioned in Conventions.

1891 First Constitutional Convention is held in Sydney.

1897–98 Constitutional Conventions held in Adelaide, Sydney and Melbourne.

1901 Australia becomes a nation when the Constitution of Australia comes into force.

1912 David Unaipon calls for Ngarrindjeri autonomy over the Point Macleay reserve.

1924 Australian Aboriginal Progressive Association (AAPA) is formed in Sydney.

1926 David Unaipon calls for the establishment of an Aboriginal state.

1927 Fred Maynard calls for abolition of protection and control of Aboriginal affairs.

1933 Yorta Yorta man William Cooper petitions King George VI seeking intervention including representation in federal Parliament. The Commonwealth did not send it on to the King. Burraga Joe Anderson calls for Indigenous representation in the federal Parliament.

1934 David Unaipon urges Commonwealth to take over Aboriginal affairs from the States.

1936 Torres Strait maritime strike which directly leads to Queensland government establishing Island councils that give them political representation and authority and some power.

1937 Yorta Yorta man William Cooper petitions King George VI for representation in Parliament.

1938 The Australian Aborigines' League and the Aborigines Progressive Association hold a 'Day of Mourning' on 26 January, calling for Commonwealth control of Indigenous affairs and a national policy.

1949 Secretary of Australia Aborigines' League Doug Nicholls writes to Prime Minister Ben Chifley seeking representation of Aboriginal people in the federal Parliament.

1958 Federal Council for Aboriginal Advancement is created (renamed in 1964 as the Federal Council for the Advancement of Aborigines and Torres Strait Islanders).

1962 Indigenous Australians granted the right to vote in federal elections.

1963 Yolngu Nation send the Yirrkala Bark Petitions to the Parliament objecting to the excision of land from their reserve for mining. They were not consulted and 'fear their needs and interests will be completely ignored as they have been ignored in the past'.

1966 Vincent Lingiari and Dexter Daniels lead their people in a walk-off at Wave Hill station, NT, to fight for wages, land rights and self-determination.

1967 A referendum is successfully held with the highest 'Yes' vote in Australian history (90.77 per cent) to amend section 51(xxvi) of the Constitution to grant legislative power over Aboriginal people to the federal Parliament and to delete section 127 of the Constitution, thereby removing the prohibition on Aboriginal people being counted in reckoning the numbers of the people of the Commonwealth.

1971 Northern Territory Supreme Court rules against Yolngu land rights claim in the first significant land rights case in Australia.

1972 The Larrakia Petition is signed by hundreds of Indigenous people, calling for land rights and political representation.

1973 National Aboriginal Consultative Committee (NACC) is established and later replaced in 1977 with the National Aboriginal Conference (NAC).

1973 Whitlam government establishes a royal commission to examine ways to recognise Aboriginal land rights.

1975 *Racial Discrimination Act* enacted by the federal Parliament.

1976 Commonwealth uses its constitutional power to legislate land rights in the Northern Territory.

1977 Fraser government creates the National Aboriginal Conference.

1979 National Aboriginal Conference calls for a treaty to be negotiated between Indigenous people and the Commonwealth following nationwide consultations with Aboriginal and Torres Strait Islander communities.

1983 Senate Standing Committee on Legal and Constitutional Affairs hands down its report *Two Hundred Years Later* . . . which recommends the government consider a treaty. The committee also recommends the insertion into the Constitution of a provision 'which would confer a broad power on the Commonwealth to enter into a compact with representatives of the Aboriginal people'.

1988 A second bark petition is presented to Prime Minister Bob Hawke by Galarrwuy Yunupingu. The Barunga Statement calls for recognition of Aboriginal rights and for a national elected Aboriginal and Islander organisation to oversee Aboriginal and Islander affairs, and for the Commonwealth to negotiate a treaty.

1989 The federal Parliament creates a new independent statutory body, the Aboriginal and Torres Strait Islander Commission (ATSIC), after an extensive consultation period including 500 meetings with 14 500 people.

1991 Australia commences a decade of statutory 'reconciliation', with the federal Parliament enacting a law establishing the Council for Aboriginal Reconciliation.

1992 The High Court hands down the *Mabo* case, in which it recognises native title and rejects the idea that Australia was *terra nullius*, or no man's land, at the time of British settlement. Prime Minister Paul Keating makes the Redfern Speech acknowledging the history of dispossession in Australia.

1993 Parliament legislates native title into law after months of tough negotiations. Keating promises compensation where Indigenous peoples are not able to claim native title by creating a land fund and a Social Justice Package.

1995 ATSIC delivers the *Recognition, Rights and Reform* report affirming community aspirations to constitutional recognition in light of *Mabo*. The Social Justice Package remains unimplemented.

1997 Human Rights and Equal Opportunity Commission tables the *Bringing Them Home* report, which examines the former practice of separating Aboriginal and Torres Strait Islander children from their families. The report recommends an official government apology to the Stolen Generations. Prime Minister John Howard refuses to do so.

1998 The High Court hands down the *Hindmarsh Island Bridge* decision, which leaves open the possibility that section 51(xxvi) of the Constitution can be used by the

Commonwealth to impose racially discriminatory laws upon Indigenous people.

1999 Australia holds a referendum to decide whether to become a republic and to adopt a new preamble to the Constitution 'honouring Aborigines and Torres Strait Islanders, the nation's first people, for their deep kinship with their lands and for their ancient and continuing cultures which enrich the life of our country'. Australians reject both proposals.

2000 The Council for Aboriginal Reconciliation delivers its *Australian Declaration towards Reconciliation* and the *Roadmap for Reconciliation*. The report reinforces Aboriginal and Torres Strait Islander aspirations for a treaty and constitutional change.

2005 Parliament abolishes ATSIC.

2007 Days prior to the federal election, Prime Minister John Howard announces the government's intention to hold a referendum to symbolically recognise Aboriginal and Torres Strait Islander peoples in a new preamble to the Constitution.

2008 Prime Minister Kevin Rudd presents the Apology to the Stolen Generations. The Australia 2020 Summit is held, with the final report noting the 'strong view that recognition of Aboriginal and Torres Strait Islander peoples' rights needs to be included in the body of the Constitution, not just in the Preamble'. The Prime Minister is presented with a Statement of Intent from Yolngu and Bininj leaders, who express their desire for constitutional protection for traditional land and cultural rights.

2010 Prime Minister Julia Gillard establishes the Expert Panel on the Recognition of Aboriginal and Torres Strait Islander Peoples in the Constitution.

2012 The Expert Panel hands down its report. There is strong support for constitutional recognition. The panel recommends a new race power with words of recognition, removing the remaining clauses that enable racial discrimination and a non-discrimination clause.

2013 The Gillard government, with support from the Opposition, passes the *Aboriginal and Torres Strait Islander Peoples Recognition Act 2013*, to provide an interim form of recognition of Aboriginal people.

2014 Parliament forms a joint select parliamentary committee, chaired by Ken Wyatt and Nova Peris, to advance the work of the Expert Panel.

2015 Indigenous leaders meet with Prime Minister Malcolm Turnbull and Opposition Leader Bill Shorten at Kirribilli House and issue the Kirribilli Statement. In response, the Prime Minister and Opposition Leader establish the Referendum Council.

2016–17 The Referendum Council runs 12 First Nations Regional Dialogues to discuss options for constitutional reform, and to ensure that Aboriginal decision-making is at the heart of the reform process.

2017 The National Constitutional Convention is held at Uluru, which ratifies the decision-making of the Regional Dialogues. The Uluru Statement from the Heart is issued to the Australian people. It calls for a constitutionally entrenched First Nations Voice to

Parliament, and a Makarrata commission to oversee a process of treaty-making and truth-telling. The Referendum Council hands down its final report, which endorses the Uluru Statement from the Heart and its call for Voice, Treaty and Truth. The Turnbull government rejects the call for a Voice to Parliament.

2018 A Joint Select Committee of Parliament to consider the work of the Referendum Council, chaired by Patrick Dodson and Julian Leeser, undertakes its work. In its final report, it finds the Voice is the only viable recognition proposal and recommends that the government 'initiate a process of co-design [of the Voice] with Aboriginal and Torres Strait Islander peoples'.

2019 Minister for Indigenous Australians Ken Wyatt announces a 'co-design' process to determine the structure and functions of the Voice.

2021 Final report released of the Indigenous Voice co-design process proposing an integrated system of Local and Regional Voices and a National Voice.

2022 Albanese Labor government elected and commits to implementing the Uluru Statement from the Heart.

2023 Voice referendum held.

1

MAKING THE CONSTITUTION

Aboriginal and Torres Strait Islander peoples have lived on the Australian continent and its islands for more than 60000 years. They are recognised as having the oldest continuous culture on the planet. They speak of their ancestors as travellers of the continent during the Creation. The Creation forms the basis of Aboriginal law, which is passed down through song, dance, rock and sand painting, language and oral explanations of myth. Before the arrival of the British, Aboriginal and Torres Strait Islander society included sophisticated political, social and cultural organisation, including trading networks and a complex system of governance, justice and decision-making. They were custodians of the 'biggest estate on earth', caring for 7.7 million square kilometres of land, which their law prescribed that they leave 'as they found it'.[1]

Several European explorers reached the Australian coast, but it was not until Captain James Cook of England in 1770 that any sought to claim the land. Cook arrived on the east coast of Australia with the following instructions from the British Navy: 'You are also, with the consent of the natives, to take possession of Convenient Situations in the

Country in the Name of the King of Great Britain'.[2] Cook was not to take the lands by force. He had been told by James Douglas, President of the Royal Society sponsoring the scientific voyage, that if any people were encountered, they were 'in the strictest sense of the word, the legal possessors of the several Regions they inhabit … Conquest over such people can give no just title'.[3]

Cook encountered Aboriginal people during his voyage. However, without their consent, on 22 August 1770, on Bedanug Island off the south-western tip of Cape York, he claimed possession of the eastern Australian coastline for King George III. Cook called this new territory 'New South Wales'.

The British resolved to use their new territory of New South Wales as a convict settlement due to the growing number of people in their jails. These were full to overflowing as the agricultural revolution forced small farmers and poor labourers off the land and into the city where many engaged in crimes such as stealing for food. In 1786, Captain Arthur Phillip was appointed as the first governor and commander-in-chief of New South Wales.

Phillip travelled to New South Wales with the First Fleet, arriving in Botany Bay on 18 January 1788. He carried no instructions requiring him to seek the consent of Aboriginal people, only to 'open an intercourse with the natives, and to conciliate their affections, enjoining all our subjects to live in amity and kindness with them'.[4] On 26 January 1788, Phillip landed in Sydney Cove and planted the Union Jack, proclaiming New South Wales as a British colony. There was no ceding of sovereignty by the Aboriginal people. As described by the bipartisan Expert

Panel that in 2012 reported on Indigenous constitutional recognition:

> It follows that ultimately the basis of settlement in Australia is and always has been the exertion of force by and on behalf of the British Crown. No-one asked permission to settle. No-one consented, no-one ceded. Sovereignty was not passed from the Aboriginal peoples by any actions of legal significance voluntarily taken by or on behalf of them.[5]

As the colony of New South Wales developed, the legal status of the continent's first peoples remained unclear. At best, the English governors were instructed to conciliate with and protect the Aboriginal 'natives' and maintain friendly relations. What actually occurred is that Indigenous peoples were progressively forced off their lands with violence and without negotiation or compensation as the colony expanded.

The period of conciliation with Aboriginal people did not last long. From the earliest days, 'many convicts and marines stole from the Aborigines their fishing and hunting tackle, their women and sometimes their lives, just as the British government, in the person of Arthur Phillip, had already stolen their land'.[6] An inability to communicate also exacerbated cultural differences. The colonists 'failed to comprehend the reciprocal obligations set up by the Aborigines. They interpreted Aboriginal attempts to enforce those obligations – by helping themselves to British goods, and later, attacking those who refused to reciprocate – as casual pilfering and treacherous violence'.[7]

The views of the early settlers about Aboriginal people varied. There were competing theories of race and changing theories about racial equality during the late 18th and early 19th centuries. While racial equality found support in the Enlightenment and in Christianity and therefore influenced some of the early settlers, these ideas increasingly clashed with the economic aspirations of the arrivals and the resistance of Aboriginal populations to dispossession on the frontier. The deaths of many thousands of Aboriginal people at the hands of British settlers and the Australian-born settlers associated with the economic and political development of Australia have become known as 'the Killing Times' or 'Frontier Wars'. The first record of resistance by an Aboriginal group was in May 1788 around Sydney and continued until the 1930s, including the Coniston Massacre in 1928 in the Northern Territory.

These conflicts occurred because the settlers wanted to exploit the land for urban expansion and the development of pastoral and other industries, and Aboriginal people were occupying those lands. The colonists continually required new land, which involved the settlers removing Aboriginal people from their country forcibly or through killing. As these conflicts took place, theories of racial hierarchy became increasingly popular. Settlers took comfort in the fiction that Aboriginal people were inferior, something that was supported by scientific and anthropological thinking from North America and Europe.

In 1803, the colony of Van Diemen's Land (later named Tasmania) was established and Lieutenant-Governor David Collins arrived with soldiers, convicts and free colonists with instructions to conciliate with the natives. Despite this, conflict began immediately as a result of the contest for land and resources. From 1813, exploration of inland Australia also continued and the colonists expanded rapidly, including into southern Queensland and central South Australia. Violence again ensued, much of it authorised by the state, as evidenced by Governor Lachlan Macquarie's Proclamation in 1816, which authorised reprisals against Aboriginal people. The law was used to validate massacres and also reflected the uncertain legal status of Aboriginal people: 'For the first fifty years the colonial legal system had trouble deciding whether the Aborigines should be treated as subjects of the Crown or foreign enemies who could be hunted down in reprisal raids and shot'.[8]

Towards Federation

The first convicts were sent to Sydney, and later to Van Diemen's Land, Port Macquarie, Moreton Bay and Norfolk Island. From the outset, convicts were the majority population of the British colony and thus the primary source of labour. Over time, free settlers also arrived and convicts began to work for them as well as the early landholders; indeed, a squatting movement saw settlers begin to expand throughout south-eastern Australia and the pastoral economy developed quickly. Squatting is an unlawful way of occupying land, but over time governments granted leases to many of these people.

As a consequence, the colonies began to expand across the continent. In 1823, the British Parliament separated the administration of Van Diemen's Land from New South

Wales and granted both colonies a Legislative Council. Then, from 1825 to 1859, the remainder of the settlements emerged as the separate self-governing colonies of Western Australia, South Australia, Queensland and Victoria.

The grant of self-government to the Australian colonies fostered the idea that they could join together to form a new nation. This movement towards Federation was driven by a number of factors, including fear of common enemies, concern for immigration and inter-colonial trade and commerce, and an emerging sense of nationalism.

The Federation movement began in earnest with a speech by Henry Parkes, the Premier of New South Wales. In 1889, at Tenterfield, he called for the colonies to 'unite and create a great national government for all Australia'.[9] He then wrote to the other colonial premiers proposing a meeting to discuss a constitution for the new nation, at which he famously remarked that 'the crimson thread of kinship runs through us all'. By this he referred to common racial and British heritage of the colonists as the basis upon which the new nation might be founded.

Parkes initiated a decade of conventions and public debate, which culminated in a Constitution and the Australian Federation in 1901. The Constitution was drafted at two Constitutional Conventions. The main issues at the Conventions were the financial and trade issues arising from Federation, and how best to weigh the interests of the small states against those of the more populous states in the new federal Parliament. Customs duties, tariffs and the capacity of the upper house of the new federal Parliament to veto money bills were of far greater concern to the Convention delegates than the rights of Aboriginal and Torres Strait

Islander peoples. Indeed, no Indigenous person was present at either Convention, nor did any delegate seek to represent their interests.

Indigenous peoples had made demands for greater representation and involvement in colonial governance. From the 1840s, they petitioned the Crown against their brutal treatment by the British. For example, in 1846, Tasmanian Aboriginal people on Flinders Island petitioned Queen Victoria, and in 1881, Yorta Yorta men living on the Maloga Mission sent a petition to the Governor of New South Wales asking for land.

Led by William Barak, the people of Coranderrk, a reserve in south central Victoria, initiated several deputations to the colonial government in Melbourne. Petitions were also sent in the 1870s and 1880s, and in 1881 this led to the Parliamentary Coranderrk Inquiry. This was the only occasion in Victoria in the 19th century on which an official commission examined Indigenous demands for land and self-determination.

Despite all of this, the process of drafting a constitution for the new nation continued without Indigenous input. The first Convention was held in Sydney in 1891 and was attended by representatives of the colonial parliaments. The draft constitution adopted by the 1891 Convention was to be put to a referendum in each colony, with a view to it being enacted for Australia by the United Kingdom Parliament. The proposal faltered when it lapsed in New South Wales without having gone to a referendum.

The process began afresh in 1895. The premiers of the colonies agreed to establish a popularly elected Convention to produce a further draft constitution to be put to the people in each colony at a referendum. This Convention met in Adelaide and Sydney in 1897, and in Melbourne in 1898. Popularly elected representatives were sent by New South Wales, South Australia, Tasmania and Victoria. Queensland was not represented at the Convention, and Western Australia sent parliamentary representatives rather than popularly elected delegates.

Rather than making a new start, the delegates to the 1897–98 Convention revised the draft constitution endorsed by the 1891 Convention. Under the leadership of Edmund Barton – later Australia's first prime minister and one of the first members of the High Court – the Convention refined the document to incorporate later compromises. This revised draft was put to the people of New South Wales, South Australia, Tasmania and Victoria. No referendum was held in Queensland or Western Australia. The draft constitution received majority support in each of the four colonies holding referendums, but was nevertheless deemed a failure in New South Wales because the number of people that voted for the draft did not reach the minimum of 80 000 required for success by the New South Wales Parliament.

The draft constitution was then amended at a conference in 1899 attended by the premiers of all six colonies. In 1899 and 1900 it was again put to the voters in the colonies, this time also in Queensland and Western Australia. On this occasion, the draft constitution was supported by a majority of voters in each colony. Large sections of the community were excluded from voting, including most women and many Aboriginal people. Women were able to vote for or against the draft constitution only in South Australia and Western Australia, while Aboriginal people were able to vote in New South Wales, South Australia, Tasmania and Victoria. However, even where Aboriginal people had a legal entitlement to vote, there is no evidence that they were able to or encouraged to do so. Just as they were absent from every step in the drafting of Australia's Constitution, so too did they play no meaningful role in endorsing the document.

After the referendums of 1899 and 1900, a delegation representing the Australian colonies was sent to London to have the draft constitution enacted by the British Parliament. In the absence of a revolution or other severing of ties with Britain, the Imperial Parliament still exercised ultimate authority over the Australian colonies. It was thus the source of power to which colonists turned to bring about the new Federation.

A Bill containing the draft constitution was introduced into the House of Commons. It completed its passage through the Imperial Parliament on 5 July 1900, was assented to by Queen Victoria on 9 July 1900 and came into force on 1 January 1901 as the *Commonwealth of Australia Constitution Act 1900*. Section 9 of the Act reads, 'The Constitution of the Commonwealth shall be as follows', and thereafter contains the entire text of the Australian Constitution.

The failure to include Aboriginal and Torres Strait Islander peoples in the move to Federation and the drafting of Australia's Constitution reflected how the colonists perceived them. There were a variety of positive anthropological and scientific opinions about Indigenous people, influenced by developments such as the end of slavery in 1833 throughout the British empire and the 'upsurge of ...

humanitarian sentiment in England'.[10] Despite this, a view took hold between 1850 and 1890 that Aboriginal people were a 'dying race', meaning that it was not expected that they would survive British settlement. This confounded the British Colonial Office, which was aware of the frontier massacres and maintained a desire to protect the Aborigines.

The dying race theory had a number of different meanings. It was primarily influenced by social Darwinism and the idea of 'survival of the fittest', but also had Christian connotations of doomed souls. Frontier killings and dispersals meant Aboriginal population numbers were dwindling, such that the dying race theory corresponded with local conditions. This was certainly influential in Tasmania, where massacres had resulted in the near extinction of Aboriginal people. Such thinking was one reason why the framers of the Australian Constitution made no effort to include Aboriginal peoples in the new political settlement.

By the time of the 1890s Conventions, the race theories that provided a justification for the dispossession of Aboriginal peoples had taken hold more generally and were also applied to other groups. Prior to Federation, many colonies had racially discriminatory employment laws. Maintaining these laws was a high priority and the framers were driven by a desire to maintain race-based distinctions. For example, they rejected the idea of inserting human rights into the Constitution because of fears that this might protect, as citizens, 'Chinamen, Japanese, Hindoos, and other barbarians' in securing employment.[11]

The text of the Constitution

The Constitution brought about a system of government for the new Australian nation based upon notions of representative and responsible government. It incorporated a separation of powers by which the courts could act as an independent check upon Parliament and the executive government. The document also reflected the views and values of the framers about Aboriginal people and the people of other races.

The preamble to the British Act that brought about the Australian Constitution speaks of the values that underlie the document and the process leading to its creation. On the other hand, no mention is made of the long history of Aboriginal and Torres Strait Islander peoples on the Australian continent. The preamble states:

> WHEREAS the people of New South Wales, Victoria, South Australia, Queensland, and Tasmania, humbly relying on the blessing of Almighty God, have agreed to unite in one indissoluble Federal Commonwealth under the Crown of the United Kingdom of Great Britain and Ireland, and under the Constitution hereby established:
>
> And whereas it is expedient to provide for the admission into the Commonwealth of other Australasian Colonies and possessions of the Queen:

> Be it therefore enacted by the Queen's most Excellent
> Majesty, by and with the advice and consent of the
> Lords Spiritual and Temporal, and Commons, in this
> present Parliament assembled, and by the authority of
> the same, as follows ... [12]

These words do not mention the people of Western Australia
because they only agreed to join the Federation after the
preamble had been drafted.

The text of the 1901 Constitution made two references
to Aboriginal people. Section 127 provided:

> In reckoning the numbers of the people of the
> Commonwealth, or of a State or other part of the
> Commonwealth, aboriginal natives shall not be
> counted.[13]

Section 127 was adopted to stop Western Australia and
Queensland from using their large Aboriginal populations
to gain extra seats in the federal Parliament and a higher
share of federal tax revenue. This reflected the view that
Aboriginal people should not be counted in determining
electoral representation and were not deserving of a share
of government income. Expressing the fringe status of
Aboriginal people of the time, Barton argued that it would
'not be considered fair to include the aborigines in population
counts'.[14] The fact that Aboriginal people were excluded
so readily and without further debate at the Conventions
reveals much about how they were viewed at the time.

This section operated in tandem with section 25 of the
Constitution. Section 25 contemplated that the states would

continue to prevent people of certain races from voting at their elections. It provided that, where this occurred, the races so excluded could not be counted in the population of that state that would be used to determine the state's representation in the federal Parliament.

Aboriginal people were also further marginalised in a new power granted to the Commonwealth Parliament. Section 51(xxvi), known as the 'races power', permitted the making of federal laws for:

> The people of any race, other than the aboriginal race in any State, for whom it is deemed necessary to make special laws.[15]

The exclusion of Aboriginal people from this power meant that laws for them were to be made instead by the states.

The races power was inserted into the Constitution to enable the federal Parliament to pass laws that discriminate against the people of any race, other than the Aboriginal race. It was to allow the Commonwealth to pass the sort of laws already in existence prior to Federation aimed at 'the Indian, Afghan, and Syrian hawkers; the Chinese miners, laundrymen, market gardeners, and furniture manu-facturers; the Japanese settlers and Kanaka plantation labourers of Queensland, and the various coloured races employed in the pearl fisheries of Queensland and Western Australia'.[16] In explaining the reasoning for this power, Sir Samuel Griffith, who later became the first Chief Justice of the High Court, observed:

> What I have had more particularly in my own mind
> was the immigration of coolies from British India,
> or any eastern people subject to civilised powers …
> I maintain that no state should be allowed, because
> the federal parliament did not choose to make a law
> on the subject, to allow the state to be flooded by such
> people as I have referred to.[17]

Similarly, Barton suggested that such a power was needed
to enable the Commonwealth to 'regulate the affairs of the
people of coloured or inferior races who are in the Commonwealth'.[18] Summarising the effect of the power, John Quick
and Robert Garran, the authors of the authoritative text on
the Constitution at the time of its enactment, wrote:

> It enables the Parliament to deal with the people
> of any alien race after they have entered the
> Commonwealth; to localise them within defined
> areas, to restrict their migration, to confine them to
> certain occupations, or to give them special protection
> and secure their return after a certain period to the
> country whence they came.[19]

Some delegates spoke strongly against such a power. Josiah
Symon, a former Attorney-General of South Australia,
argued: 'It is monstrous to put a brand on these people when
you admit them. It is degrading to us and our citizenship
to do such a thing. If we say they are fit to be admitted
amongst us, we ought not to degrade them by putting on
them a brand of inferiority'.[20] However, lest it be thought
that section 51(xxvi) might confer any protection from

racial discrimination, Quick and Garran continued: 'On the contrary, it would seem that by sub-sec xxvi the federal Parliament will have power to pass special and discriminating laws relating to "the people of any race," and that such laws could not be challenged on the ground of unconstitutionality'.[21]

Despite the races power being the subject of extensive discussion, the Convention debates are silent as to why Aboriginal people were excluded from the section. Perhaps, to use the language of the time, it was the thought that the states, and not the Commonwealth, should 'smooth the dying pillow' of Aboriginal people.

Tasmanian Attorney-General Andrew Inglis Clark proposed that the new Constitution guarantee every citizen due process of law and the equal protection of the law. He based this upon the Fourteenth Amendment to the United States Constitution. This might have prevented the states from enacting and maintaining racially discriminatory laws.

The proposal for a due process clause was problematic in Australia because racially discriminatory laws excluding people from Asia and the Pacific from seeking a mining licence and other areas of employment were seen as normal across the states. The early Australian colonies openly espoused the racist sentiment that was so evident in their laws. The framers wanted to preserve such laws. The most outspoken on this was the premier of Western Australia, Sir John Forrest, who said: 'We have made a law that no Asiatic or African alien can get a miner's right or do any gold mining. Does the Convention wish to take [that] away from us …?'[22] He went on:

It is of no use for us to shut our eyes to the fact that there is a great feeling all over Australia against the introduction of coloured persons. It goes without saying that we do not like to talk about it, but still it is so. I do not want this clause to pass in a shape which would undo what is about to be done in most of the colonies, and what has already been done in Western Australia, in regard to that class of persons.[23]

Ultimately, a compromise was fashioned, with future High Court Justice Henry Higgins proposing a clause that became section 117 of the Constitution. Rather than protecting against racial discrimination or providing equality under the law, this provision states that a person resident in one state cannot be 'subject in any other State to any disability or discrimination which would not be equally applicable to him if he were ... resident in such other State'. For example, a person residing in Queensland could not be denied a job in New South Wales because of their Queensland residency. The result was a very narrow form of protection. According to Higgins, this 'would allow Sir John Forrest ... to have his law with regard to Asiatics not being able to obtain miners' rights in Western Australia. There is no discrimination there based on residence or citizenship; it is simply based on colour and race'.[24]

The new Commonwealth Parliament

After the Constitution came into force, Australia's first general election was held on 29 and 30 March 1901. It led to a government being formed by Barton, and the first sitting of the new federal Parliament on 9 May. The importance of race-based distinctions became immediately apparent. One of the first pieces of legislation enacted by the new Parliament was the *Immigration Restriction Act 1901*, which prohibited the immigration into Australia of any person who, when asked by an officer, was unable to 'write out at dictation and sign in the presence of the officer a passage of fifty words in length in an European language directed by the officer'.[25] This was the means by which the White Australia policy was implemented.

Introducing the Bill, Prime Minister Barton argued:

> I do not think either that the doctrine of the equality of man was really ever intended to include racial equality. There is no racial equality. There is that basic inequality. These races are, in comparison with white races – I think no one wants convincing of this fact – unequal and inferior. The doctrine of the equality of man was never intended to apply to the equality of the Englishman and the Chinaman. There is deep-set difference, and we see no prospect and no promise of its ever being effaced. Nothing in this world can put these two races upon an equality. Nothing we can do by cultivation, by refinement, or by anything else will make some races equal to others.[26]

On Aboriginal people, Alfred Deakin, Australia's first federal Attorney-General and second Prime Minister, said:

> Little more than a hundred years ago Australia was a Dark Continent in every sense of the term. There was not a white man within its borders. In another century the probability is that Australia will be a White Continent with not a black or even dark skin amongst its inhabitants. The aboriginal race has died out in the South and is dying fast in the North and West even where most gently treated. Other races are to be excluded by legislation if they are tinted to any degree.[27]

Soon after, Parliament passed a law setting out who could vote in federal elections. The *Commonwealth Franchise Act 1902* was progressive for its time in extending the franchise to women. It had also been proposed that the franchise encompass Aboriginal people, but this was strongly resisted and ultimately defeated. Among its opponents were Isaac Isaacs, later a judge of the High Court and Australia's first native-born Governor-General, who suggested that Aboriginal people 'have not the intelligence, interest, or capacity' to vote.[28] Similarly, Higgins thought it 'utterly inappropriate … [to] ask them to exercise an intelligent vote'.[29]

As finally enacted, the law denied federal voting rights to every 'aboriginal native of Australia … unless so entitled under section forty-one of the Constitution'.[30] Section 41 says that a person is guaranteed the vote in federal elections if they can vote for the more numerous House of their state Parliament. However, where Aboriginal people were entitled to vote in a state, such as South Australia, a vote in federal elections was in practice still denied to them. The ban on Aboriginal people voting in federal elections continued until 1962. Even then, full equality at federal elections did not occur until 1983, when the law was amended to make enrolment for and voting in federal elections compulsory for Indigenous people, as it had been for decades for other Australians.

A growing mood for change

Today, when the High Court interprets the Constitution, it turns to the records of the Convention debates during the 1890s to understand the intention of the drafters. Yet, there is no record of Aboriginal and Torres Strait Islander peoples playing any role in the drafting of the Constitution or the process that led to the creation of the Australian nation. Nor did they take part in the delegation that travelled to Britain to have that document enacted. Nor is there any record of Indigenous people being consulted about this, or their consent being sought to bring about a new nation on their ancestral lands. Instead, the Constitution was drafted to exclude Aboriginal people, who many of the colonists viewed as a 'dying race'.

Over time, frontier violence gave way to a new situation for Aboriginal people in Australia. Excluded from the political settlement that brought about the new nation, Aboriginal people found themselves forced onto missions and reserves. The Constitution meant that responsibility for their welfare fell to the states, which initiated what is known as the 'Protection Era'.

The word 'protection' was a euphemism for a period that ushered in a system of segregation on the basis of race. Aboriginal people were herded off country, often at gunpoint, and placed onto designated parcels of land often surrounded by wire to separate them from mainstream society. The Protection Era is distinguished by special, seemingly benevolent legislation aimed at protecting Aboriginal people from the 'worst effects of contact with Europeans', including diseases and violence.[31] However, these laws were draconian. They forced Aboriginal people off country to live on state- and missionary-run reserves. Every aspect of their lives was regulated, from marriage, employment and freedom of movement, to regulation of their work and how pay from that work was to be spent. The era was characterised by overtly discriminatory laws in which Aboriginal people were denied equality in almost every aspect of their lives.

One of the worst features of the Protection Era was the removal of children from their families – known as the Stolen Generations. This was often justified by invoking the 'protection' of Aboriginal and Torres Strait Islander peoples, but the forcible removal of children was intended to weaken Aboriginal culture and kinship and to debilitate many manifestations of culture such as language and ceremony. It also led to social and medical issues arising as a consequence of removal. However, this treatment did not go unnoticed. A growing sense of injustice arising from the treatment of Aboriginal and Torres Strait Islander peoples led many Australians to argue for change, including to the Constitution.

2

THE 1967 REFERENDUM

On 27 May 1967, Australians voted Yes to change the Constitution. They did so in overwhelming numbers (90.77 per cent) never seen in Australia – and not seen since. Exactly what this referendum achieved has long been the subject of debate and misunderstanding. Indeed, the vote has attained somewhat of a mythical status that far exceeds the legal changes it brought about. Even to this day, it is said that the referendum meant that Aboriginal people became Australian citizens, or that they got the right to vote. The referendum achieved neither of these things.

The changes to the Constitution brought about by the referendum were modest, and had more to do with altering Australia's federal architecture than creating new rights for Aboriginal and Torres Strait Islander peoples. The referendum deleted two sets of words from the Constitution. First, it removed an exclusion from the races power in section 51(xxvi) that had prevented the federal Parliament from enacting laws for Aboriginal people. Second, it repealed section 127, which had prevented Aboriginal people from being included in 'reckoning the numbers of the people of the Commonwealth'.

Both provisions referred to Aboriginal people in negative ways, either by way of removing them as a subject of federal power, or by excluding them from the count of the people of the Commonwealth used for determining representation in the federal Parliament. The deletions did not, however, grant Aboriginal people any new rights or recognition. In terms of recognition, the referendum removed the only references to Aboriginal peoples in the document, leaving nothing in their place. The referendum also extended the races power to them without indicating that the power should only be used for their benefit. This opened the possibility that the power might be used to discriminate against them.

Modern recollections of the 1967 referendum tend to overlook the fact that Australians also voted that day on another proposal to change the Constitution. A second, unsuccessful, idea was put to the people that would have removed the requirement in the Constitution that the House of Representatives have twice as many members as the Senate. It was this second proposal, seeking to break the link, or 'nexus' as it was called, between the houses of Parliament, that attracted the lion's share of public debate. This proposal, rather than the referendum on Indigenous peoples, was the main focus for most of Australia's political leaders, including the government of the day.

Decades of debate

The 1967 referendum was the product of decades of agitation and advocacy by Aboriginal and Torres Strait

Islander peoples and their supporters. The idea that the Commonwealth should have power over Aboriginal peoples can be traced back to shortly after Federation, when the idea was suggested as a means of responding to the 'problem' of Aboriginal people being a 'dying race'. For example, in 1913, a committee on Aboriginal welfare, established by the Australasian Association for the Advancement of Science, argued that 'the Aboriginal problem will only be solved when all that is left of the race is made a single and National responsibility and cared for in a National way'. The committee argued that this could create a 'national sentiment of sympathy and pity ... towards this unfortunate race whom we have dispossessed'.[1]

Similarly, in the late 1920s, the Association for the Protection of the Native Races of Australasia and Polynesia argued that the federal and not the state tier of government should have responsibility for passing laws for Aboriginal peoples:

> The method of relying upon State and Colonial
> Governments has been tried from the earliest days
> of colonisation, and has undeniably failed ... It is
> a recognised political principle that the wider the
> area from which the governing power is derived, the
> larger the task set, the wider and more statesmanlike
> the policy is likely to be. It follows as a corollary
> that the Federal government is likely to deal with
> the whole problem more adequately than the State
> Governments.[2]

The dissenting report to the 1929 Royal Commission on the Constitution agreed, and recommended that the Commonwealth should have responsibility for Indigenous peoples.

Meanwhile, Indigenous peoples were engaged in advocacy for their rights and self-determination. The Australian Aboriginal Progressive Association (AAPA) was formed in Sydney in 1924. It called for an Aboriginal board to sit below the Commonwealth government, and for Indigenous self-determination. In 1927, the AAPA launched a manifesto that sought: 'The control of Aboriginal affairs, apart from common law rights, shall be vested in a board of management comprised of capable educated Aboriginals under a chairman to be appointed by the government'.

In 1933, Joe Anderson – also known as King Burraga – from the Salt Pan Creek on the Georges River, New South Wales, called for representation in the federal Parliament, and a corroboree for all Aboriginal people in New South Wales to organise a petition to the King. Four years later, in 1937, William Cooper, a Yorta Yorta man and inaugural Secretary of the Australian Aborigines' League, organised a petition to the King, demanding Aboriginal representation in Parliament. Cooper had spent several years gathering a large number of signatures on the petition, from all around the country. The Australian government acknowledged receipt of the petition, but refused to forward it to the King.

A few months later, on 26 January 1938, the Australian Aborigines' League, together with the Aborigines Progressive Association, initiated a 'Day of Mourning', calling for Commonwealth control of Indigenous affairs and a national policy. Speakers included renowned Aboriginal leaders and activists: Jack Patten, who was the first president of the Aborigines Progressive Association; William Ferguson, a Wiradjuri man who founded the Aborigines Progressive Association; Doug Nicholls, a Yorta Yorta man; and Pearl Gibbs, a Ngemba or Muruwari woman and a member of the Aborigines Progressive Association. The organisers of the Day of Mourning also arranged the first ever Indigenous deputation to the Prime Minister. They presented him with a Ten-Point Plan for Indigenous equality. Fundamental to this was citizenship rights. The demand was phrased as:

> WE, representing THE ABORIGINES OF AUSTRALIA, assembled in conference at the Australian Hall, Sydney, on the 26th day of January, 1938, this being the 150th Anniversary of the Whiteman's seizure of our country, HEREBY MAKE PROTEST against the callous treatment of our people by the whitemen during the past 150 years, AND WE APPEAL to the Australian nation of today to make new laws for the education and care of Aborigines, we ask for a new policy which will raise our people TO FULL CITIZEN STATUS and EQUALITY WITHIN THE COMMUNITY.[3]

However, the Constitution remained a barrier, as it precluded the Commonwealth from legislating about Indigenous peoples. In 1944, the Curtin government unsuccessfully sought power over Indigenous peoples in the failed Post-War Reconstruction and Democratic Rights referendum. Despite this setback, the debate stepped up a notch in the late 1940s and 1950s, including through the advocacy of Aboriginal organisations such as the Aborigines Progressive Association and the Australian Aborigines' League. This reflected developments not only in Australia, but internationally, such as the Universal Declaration of Human Rights, which, in 1948, recognised 'the inherent dignity' and 'the equal and inalienable rights of all members of the human family'.[4]

In 1949, Indigenous returned servicemen were given the right to vote. In 1950, the House of Representatives unanimously moved a motion that the Commonwealth:

a   Exercises national responsibility for Aboriginal people and cooperates with the States.
b   Works towards the social advancement as well as the protection of Aborigines.
c   Provides additional finance and effective administration.[5]

This was accompanied by a growing sense that Aboriginal people should have the same rights as other Australians. For example, in 1957, Opposition Leader and former High Court Justice HV Evatt declared in Parliament: 'the only thing to be done with the Australian Aboriginal, full-blood or otherwise, is to give him the benefit of the same laws as apply to every other Australian'.[6]

In 1962, the vote in federal elections was extended to all Indigenous Australians, which strengthened the case for constitutional reform. It was clearly absurd for Indigenous Australians to have the vote, only for section 127 of the Constitution to deny them the right to be counted for the purposes of determining electoral districts.

Advocacy for change waxed and waned, but was finally put on the national political agenda by the efforts of many people, including civil rights campaigners Lady Jessie Street and Faith Bandler. A campaign was built upon the idea that Aboriginal people should have full rights as citizens and that their welfare should be a federal responsibility. In 1958, this led to the creation of the Federal Council for Aboriginal Advancement (renamed in 1964 as the Federal Council for the Advancement of Aborigines and Torres Strait Islanders).

Over the following decade, this organisation became the leading proponent for constitutional change and for the Yes case at the 1967 referendum. The first and primary principle of the body was that Aboriginal people should be granted 'equal citizenship with other Australian citizens'.[7] It sought this by way of repealing any federal or state legislation that discriminated against Aboriginal people and amending the Australian Constitution to give the federal Parliament the power to legislate for them. The body advocated for these changes through community and political activism, including public events, speaking tours and petitions presented to Parliament.

The movement for constitutional reform continued to make strides through the early 1960s, including through the Freedom Ride in 1965 in which 30 University of Sydney students – including Aboriginal activist Charles Perkins and future New South Wales Supreme Court Chief Justice Jim Spigelman – travelled through rural New South Wales to draw attention to discrimination against Indigenous people. That same year, Western Australia and Queensland became the last states to grant Aboriginal people the right to vote.

By 1967, there was consensus on the need for reform, both in the community and across political parties.

Despite many years of advocacy, the change to the Constitution only achieved solid political backing in the final days of the Menzies government. Prime Minister Robert Menzies had been reluctant to attempt any constitutional reform since his failure to convince the Australian people to ban the Communist Party of Australia at the 1951 referendum. Nevertheless, in 1965, his government committed to putting two questions to the people: one concerning Aboriginal peoples, and the other seeking to break the nexus between the sizes of the two Houses of federal Parliament.

Even then, there was no rush for these questions to be taken to the ballot box, and in the meantime, Menzies was succeeded as Prime Minister on Australia Day 1966 by his Treasurer, Harold Holt. Holt also took his time, and showed no special interest in the proposals. However, after winning the November 1966 general election, he kept to the Liberal Party's public commitment to put both questions to the people, and so a referendum was finally put on 27 May 1967.

The proposals put to the people

The proposal on Aboriginal peoples at the 1967 referendum included two components. Both reflected fundamental changes in Australia's idea of Aboriginal people since Federation. Neither of the 1890s Conventions that debated the Constitution had made serious mention of Indigenous people. Cast as a 'dying race', they played no meaningful role in its drafting. While the preamble to the Constitution suggests that 'the people ... have agreed to unite', it makes no mention of Aboriginal people or their occupation of the lands upon which the new nation was formed.

The operative provisions of the Constitution were also based upon the exclusion of Indigenous peoples, and even discrimination against them. As drafted in 1901, the Constitution made two references to Aboriginal people. The races power in section 51(xxvi) empowered the federal Parliament to make laws with respect to: 'The people of any race, *other than the aboriginal race in any State*, for whom it is deemed necessary to make special laws'. The words in italics meant that the power could not be used by the federal Parliament to make laws for Aboriginal peoples, as this was to be a state and not a federal responsibility. The 1967 referendum deleted the words in italics, thereby granting legislative power over Aboriginal people to the federal Parliament. The referendum did not deny the states the continuing ability to legislate for Aboriginal peoples. It simply meant that both tiers of government now had the power to do so.

The referendum also repealed section 127, which had provided: 'In reckoning the numbers of the people of the Commonwealth, or of a state or other part of the Commonwealth, aboriginal natives shall not be counted'. The section meant that Aboriginal people were not to be counted for the purpose of determining the size and distribution of electorates for the federal Parliament. Even though the section arguably only applied for electoral purposes, it had a wider impact on how Aboriginal people were counted in the national census. The Expert Panel that in 2012 reported on the constitutional recognition of Indigenous peoples described the situation in this way:

> At the first Australian census in 1911, only those 'aboriginal natives' living near white settlements were counted, and the main population tables included only those of half or less Aboriginal descent. Details of 'half-caste' (but not 'full-blood') Aboriginal people were included in the tables on race. Details of 'full-blood' Aboriginal people were included in separate tables. The practice was followed in all censuses up until 1966.[8]

This practice reflected the opinion of the Commonwealth Attorney-General at the time of the 1911 census that section 127 meant that censuses and other government publications of population figures could not include 'full-blooded Aborigines'.[9]

In electoral terms, the effect of section 127 was a substantial under-weighting of the Aboriginal and Torres Strait Islander vote. This reflected the view widely held at Federation that they were not entitled to take part in Australia's democratic processes. Well before 1967, national attitudes had changed. The ban on Aboriginal people voting in federal elections was removed in 1962. A sense had also emerged that it was no longer acceptable to have a provision in the Constitution such as section 127, which was so obviously discriminatory. Rooting out this constitutionalised discrimination was an important part of changing Australia's conception of itself as a nation.

Attitudes had also changed by this time on whether the Commonwealth should be able to make laws for Indigenous peoples. By 1967, the states were moving towards uniformity in Indigenous policy, but gaps remained. Why, it was asked, should an Indigenous person have freedom of movement in New South Wales, but upon crossing the Queensland border need permission to enter a hotel? Why did only South Australia apply internationally recognised labour standards to Indigenous employees? Above all, one issue predominated: when it came to Aboriginal disadvantage, why should the Commonwealth have all the money, but none of the responsibility?

Support for the referendum came from all quarters. Every major party and many community figures supported the change. Letters to newspapers ran almost unequivocally in favour of a Yes vote. The unique national consensus was reflected in the absence of a No campaign. Even the 'for and against' booklet sent to voters to inform them of the referendum only contained arguments for change. This was because federal law required the 'against' case in the booklet to be written by the parliamentarians who had voted against the change, and on this occasion not one parliamentarian did so.

Where there was opposition, it lay at the margins of the debate. Some argued a losing battle for state power, saying that power should remain with the states so they could fashion locally appropriate laws. Others took the opposite tack, arguing that the Commonwealth should have no power to make race-based laws at all, for that was the first step towards segregation and apartheid. Neither of these arguments had an impact. The Australian people had made up their minds to move on from the past and were swept up in the notion that voting Yes would remedy past injustices and forge a brighter path forward.

Public discussion of the referendum tended not to mention the changes to the text of the Constitution. The focus was instead on the symbolic nature of the shift. The media mostly covered the issue only in broad and positive terms. For *The Age*, for example, the question was a 'simple matter of humanity ... [and] a test of Australia's standing in the world'.[10] It said the question posed to Australians was whether they would yet recognise that 'Aborigines [should] be regarded as completely human'.[11] Other newspapers took a similar approach, with the *Sydney Morning Herald* running a front-page photo of two children, one Aboriginal and one white, gazing happily at each other as they walked down a laneway hand in hand.

The media coverage reflected the campaign run by the Yes case, both before the referendum campaign and during it. The change was portrayed in general terms as being 'Towards Equal Citizenship for Aborigines', despite the fact that, as a matter of law, Aboriginal people were included as citizens when the concept of Australian citizenship was first created by the *Nationality and Citizenship Act 1948*.

Nonetheless, the idea of attaining citizenship rights was a major part of the campaign, with leaders, such as Faith Bandler, arguing that the change would grant Aboriginal people 'full citizenship rights and nothing less'. Others used the same theme, but in more general terms, with Aboriginal leader Chicka Dixon arguing for a Yes vote because 'I want to be accepted by white Australians as a person' and because he wanted to see 'white Australians finally, after

179 years, affirming at last that they believe we are human beings'.[12] Similarly, the Federal Council for the Advancement of Aborigines and Torres Strait Islanders urged the media to encourage a Yes vote to 'Aboriginal rights' and 'to give the Aborigines full citizenship rights'.[13] One advertisement run by the Council simply exhorted 'Right Wrongs Write YES for Aborigines!' accompanied by a picture of an Aboriginal baby.

Constructing the debate in this way proved highly effective in building a compelling and emotive case for change. However, it also fuelled misconceptions around the referendum. It is no surprise, given the rhetoric used at the time and the fact that many Australians know little about their Constitution, that many people still believe today the referendum dealt with fundamental questions of justice and Aboriginal rights, such as their status as citizens and ability to vote. These misconceptions have sometimes been accompanied by the myth that the referendum overrode a Flora and Fauna Act by which Aboriginal people were treated as part of Australia's native wildlife. No such Act has ever existed.

Exaggerated ideas about the changes brought about by the 1967 referendum are a problem. They undermine understandings of our legal and democratic system, and place a barrier in the way of future constitutional change.

For example, if the 1967 referendum had already achieved the grand ideals expressed at the time, why is it necessary to hold a second referendum on the same topic? Part of the task, then, of convincing Australians to vote Yes at any contemporary referendum on constitutional recognition of Aboriginal peoples, is to first explain the limited nature of what was brought about in 1967. It is only once the modest legal scope of that referendum is understood, including the fact that it removed all references to Aboriginal people without inserting anything positive in their place, that it becomes clear that the referendum left behind unfinished business still worthy of debate today.

This unfinished business includes that the referendum did not alter provisions enabling race-based discrimination. The races power is the prime example of this. The scope of the power was extended to Aboriginal people in 1967 without altering the fact that the section was drafted to enable discrimination against people due to their race. As a result, the referendum opened the door for the power to be used to make laws beneficial or adverse to Aboriginal people. The negative possibility did not get much public attention at the time, overwhelmed as everyone was by the positive messages surrounding the referendum, including how an expanded races power could be used to enact national laws for the welfare of Aboriginal peoples. This gave rise, in the words of former Chief Justice of the High Court Robert French, to a 'tension … between these beneficial objectives and the predominantly negative discrimination envisaged by the drafters of the original provision'.[14]

Nevertheless, some people did explain at the time that the referendum could have unintended and unfortunate consequences for Aboriginal peoples. One of Australia's leading constitutional lawyers, Geoffrey Sawer, warned that 'the dubious origins of the [races power], and the dangerous potentialities of adverse discriminatory treatment which it contains' meant that 'the complete repeal of the section would be preferable to any amendment intended to extend its possible benefits to the Aborigines'.[15] Similarly, federal

Liberal parliamentarian William (Billy) Wentworth, a prominent supporter of reform and subsequently Australia's first federal Minister for Aboriginal Affairs, wrote in the *Sydney Morning Herald* in 1965 that extending the races power to Aboriginal people in this way could be a 'cure ... worse than the disease ... [as] to remove these words would subject Aborigines to potential discrimination rather than protect them from it'.[16]

Wentworth argued, instead, for replacing the entire text of the races power with a new power to make laws for 'the advancement of the Aboriginal natives of the Commonwealth of Australia', along with a new section 117A to prohibit the Commonwealth and the states from maintaining any law 'which subjects any person who has been born or naturalised within the Commonwealth of Australia to any discrimination or disability within the Commonwealth by reason of his racial origin'. In 1966, Wentworth introduced a private members Bill into Parliament to bring about these changes, but it was not passed, and the government instead proceeded with its more limited proposal.

The 1967 referendum also failed to make any change to section 25 of the Constitution, which is headed 'Provision as to races disqualified from voting'. It provides that, for the purpose of determining how many members each state shall have in the House of Representatives, 'if by the law of any State all persons of any race are disqualified from voting at elections for the more numerous House of the Parliament of the State, then, in reckoning the number of the people of the State or of the Commonwealth, persons of that race resident in that State shall not be counted'. Section 25 lowers the population count of a state if that state disqualifies people of a particular race from voting, and thus penalises it by restricting its parliamentary representation. However, in doing so, the provision acknowledges that Aboriginal and other racial groups can be so disqualified.

Attempts have been made to repeal section 25, but without success. One attempt was made at the 1967 referendum, but not as part of the proposal dealing with the races power and section 127. The proposed repeal was actually included in a second question put on the same day. The focus of that question was that voters should break the 'nexus' between the sizes of the House of Representatives and the Senate. In the Constitution, the framers set out in section 24 that the House must be, as near as practicable, twice the size of the Senate. For most of Australia's history to that point, there had been 36 Senators (six from each state) and approximately 72 members of the lower house.

In 1949, the Chifley Labor government increased the size of both Houses. The Senate was increased from 36 to 60 members and the House from 74 to 121. Despite this increase, rapid population growth meant that Australians were represented by far fewer Commonwealth parliamentarians per head of population than had been the case at Federation. In 1901, there was about one member of Parliament for every 50000 Australians; by 1967, that number was 94000.

Both major parties were reluctant to increase the size of the House because that would require a proportionate increase in the size of the Senate. Because of the Senate's system of proportional voting, the effect would be to increase the power of minor parties and possibly independents. These facts had formed the basis of a recommendation in the 1959 report of the bipartisan Joint Committee on Constitutional Review of the federal Parliament to break the nexus between the sizes of the Houses. In addition to repealing section 25, the nexus proposal sought to do three things: it would remove any link between the size of the Houses of Commonwealth Parliament; it would set a maximum number of Members of the House, being no more than one for every 85 000 Australians; and it would set a minimum number of Senators, being ten per state. The key to the proposal from the government's perspective was the first of these, the breaking of the nexus. The other two parts to the proposal were designed, ultimately unsuccessfully, to alleviate concerns that the proposal was an attack on the Senate.

For its proponents, an increase in the size of Parliament was necessary for effective representative government. The parliamentarian-to-voter ratio was said to be too low for representatives to properly respond to their constituents' needs. Not only were parliamentarians representing many more people than in the past, they were saddled with far greater responsibilities as the Commonwealth had entered into fields that had traditionally been the responsibility of the states. If there were an increase in the size of the House so that constituents could be effectively represented, the question was whether that should necessarily flow on to an increase in the size of the Senate. Should an increase on one side of the equation necessarily cause an increase on the other? For the advocates of change, the answer was No. This was the case that Harold Holt and the leaders of the Country Party (John McEwen) and Labor Opposition (Gough Whitlam) took to the people. They had the support of all 124 members of the House and 50 of the 60 members of the Senate.

Against the heavy artillery of the major parties was a motley crew of ten Senators. Most prominent were Vincent Gair, federal leader of the Democratic Labor Party (DLP), Frank McManus, Victorian DLP representative, and Reginald Wright, Tasmanian Liberal representative. They were supported by three other Liberal Senators, two Country Party Senators and two Independents. The No campaign mobilised quickly and rallied under the simple banner of 'no more politicians'. The claim was this: the only check on the size of the House is that a government wanting to expand the House must also expand the Senate. If you take away that check, they said, greed will lead to ever more politicians in Canberra. The No campaign was vigorous and effective.

Even as the press stepped up its coverage, Australians continued to suffer widespread ignorance and confusion about the proposal. Australians did not understand the word 'nexus'; nor did they understand the constitutional principle that the proposal was targeted at – the tying together of the sizes of the Senate and House. As referendum day approached, Holt targeted the No campaign. He called opponents 'childish' and spouters of prejudice and ignorance.[17] When Holt spoke on the referendum, his focus remained on the question of the nexus. Just a fifth of his key speech delivered on the night of 15 May – about two minutes – was devoted to what was known as the 'Aboriginals proposal'. The press reported that, by and large, the Aboriginals proposal was ignored by the parties.

Outcomes of the referendum

On referendum day, Australians voted in very different ways for the nexus and Aboriginals proposals. Only the latter succeeded in gaining the required national majority of Yes votes and a majority of Yes votes in a majority of the six states. The results, along with the questions put to voters, appear overleaf.[18]

As these results demonstrate, the Aboriginals proposal streaked ahead. Indeed, it recorded the highest national Yes vote for any referendum proposal ever put to the people. The change was supported overwhelmingly in every state, and nationally more than nine in ten formal votes were Yes votes. The lowest Yes vote was in Western Australia, but still more than eight in ten Western Australians supported the proposal, thereby making it the most successful referendum ever in that state. The largest No vote of any area was recorded in the Western Australian rural district of Kalgoorlie, where 8888 voters – or 29 per cent – were against the change.

The pattern Australia-wide for the Aboriginals proposal was for extremely strong Yes votes in the cities and slightly lower Yes votes in rural and regional areas. The differences in attitude between electors in regional areas, where there was a higher concentration of Indigenous people, and those in urban areas disturbed many. The referendum's success was unquestioned, but the attitudes it revealed were disappointing to some. Who, it was asked, would vote against a proposal to count Indigenous Australians in determining electoral boundaries and to give the Commonwealth power to make laws for their welfare?

Most Australians voted the opposite way for the nexus proposal. At the final count, barely four in ten Australians supported a proposal that had the approval of the three major parties, the bipartisan Joint Committee on Constitutional Review and much of the press. Only New South Wales returned a Yes vote, in its case one of 51.01 per cent. The results in the other states were disastrous for proponents. Victoria, Holt's home state, recorded a Yes vote of barely more than 30 per cent, which remains the lowest Yes vote ever recorded by that state. Tasmanians said No in a greater proportion than any other state, with close to eight in ten (76.9 per cent) voting against the reform.

The day after the referendum, Holt left to travel overseas. Rather than focusing on the extraordinary moment of national consensus recorded in the vote on the Aboriginals proposal, he focused on the failure of the nexus proposal. Rather than labelling 27 May as a victory for Aboriginal Australians, he labelled the referendum a 'victory for prejudice and misrepresentation'.[19] Holt blamed Australians: 'the majority of electors chose to ignore the advice of those to whom they normally look for guidance'.[20] The nexus proposal was also the main focus for the press. Page one of the *Sunday Herald* on 28 May recorded the Yes vote on Aboriginals in small type, while blaring in big, bold capitals: 'AUSTRALIA SAYS NO ON NEXUS'.[21]

The press had its eye on the political ramifications of the No vote for the nexus proposal, but the community campaigners who had fought the Aboriginals proposal saw things differently. Cast as a referendum that would recognise

Question 1

Do you approve the proposed law for the alteration of the Constitution entitled 'An Act to alter the Constitution so that the number of Members of the House of Representatives may be increased without necessarily increasing the number of Senators'?

State	For	%	Against	%	Informal
New South Wales	1 087 694	51.01	1 044 458	48.99	34 355
Victoria	496 826	30.87	1 112 506	69.13	21 262
Queensland	370 200	44.13	468 673	55.87	9855
South Australia	186 344	33.91	363 120	66.09	11 380
Western Australia	114 841	29.05	280 523	70.95	10 302
Tasmania	42 764	23.06	142 660	76.94	3821
National Total	2 298 669	40.25	3 411 940	59.75	90 975

Not Carried

Question 2

Do you approve the proposed law for the alteration of the Constitution entitled 'An Act to alter the Constitution so as to omit certain words relating to the people of the Aboriginal race in any state so that Aboriginals are to be counted in reckoning the population'?

State	For	%	Against	%	Informal
New South Wales	1 949 036	91.46	182 010	8.54	35 461
Victoria	1 525 026	94.68	85 611	5.32	19 957
Queensland	748 612	89.21	90 587	10.79	9529
South Australia	473 440	86.26	75 383	13.74	12 021
Western Australia	319 823	80.95	75 282	19.05	10 561
Tasmania	167 176	90.21	18 134	9.79	3935
National Total	5 183 113	90.77	527 007	9.23	91 464

Carried

Aboriginal rights and even their inherent humanity, it is no surprise that its supporters saw the outcome as a landmark in Australian history and as a defining social and political event. In this respect, the response exceeded the narrow confines of the legal changes actually brought about. Hence, Bandler has said of the result that 'we went mad with excitement',[22] while Jackie Huggins, a Bidjara/Pitjara and Biri Birri Gubba Juru woman, remembers as a young girl 'the shrieks of joy after the result was announced, laughter and a mass of tears'.[23]

Others have spoken of how it immediately changed the way Aboriginal people saw themselves within the community. In the aftermath of the referendum: 'There were black people on the streets in a way we have never seen them … People were up, had washed their children, combed their hair and got themselves up in their very best gear and walked out in the streets of Brisbane, down Queen Street where they never went.'[24] Similarly, even though Aboriginal people were legally entitled to vote in federal elections before the 1967 referendum, it was only after the referendum that many felt able and willing to exercise that right. Although the vote did not establish Aboriginal peoples as Australian citizens, as they already possessed that status, it did mean that many saw themselves in this way for the first time, and were treated by more members of the community as possessing such rights.

It is only over time that Australians have come to see the true significance of the 1967 referendum. By the time of the 40th anniversary of the referendum in 2007, the reaction to the two polls was reversed. The focus was firmly on the Yes vote cast by Australians to remove discrimination against Aboriginal peoples and enable laws to be made on their behalf. Little or no attention was paid to the nexus proposal, with many Australians not even realising that on referendum day in 1967 two votes had been cast.

It is clear with the benefit of hindsight that, beyond the legal changes brought about by the referendum, it was a watershed moment in Australia's political and social affairs. It emboldened Indigenous groups and reinforced their public advocacy. Many took strength from the overwhelming success of the poll. The unprecedented Yes vote was also interpreted as a strong mandate for the making of national laws and policy on Indigenous affairs.

Nothing, however, in the changes to the Constitution required the Commonwealth to take over authority for Aboriginal affairs. It merely gave the federal Parliament a power, like that already held by the states, to make laws in this area if it so wished. Indeed, the view of the Holt government soon after the referendum was that it had no intention of taking over responsibility in the area. Bandler commented that the government had made 'a mockery of the referendum … It is as if the electorate had never made any moral commitment to do a great deal more for Aborigines'.[25] Bandler here touched upon the political power of the referendum. The momentum created by an overwhelming vote of the Australian people in favour of Aboriginal rights and better treatment for Aboriginal peoples could not be ignored. Federal inaction was no longer possible.

This potential of the referendum was not realised until the election of the Whitlam government in 1972. It interpreted the referendum not only as providing legal power to the Commonwealth, but a political mandate to do so. This led the Whitlam and subsequent governments to exert federal authority through wide-ranging legislation in areas such as land rights, cultural heritage and ultimately native title, and also through government programs designed to overcome Indigenous disadvantage. Many of these laws and programs could have been undertaken by the Commonwealth with the powers it already had prior to the 1967 referendum, but the referendum provided the catalyst for change. It is in this sense, more than in the legal changes actually brought about, that the 1967 referendum was a turning point for Aboriginal and Torres Strait Islander peoples and their relationship with government.

3

A NEW ERA?

The success of the 1967 referendum sparked a flurry of activity in Aboriginal and Torres Strait Islander communities. Buoyed by the result, they sought to advance their agenda through federal legislation for goals such as recognising land rights. This reflected an expectation that the federal Parliament would immediately use the expanded races power to fulfil the aspirations of Indigenous peoples. The reality was very different.

Initially, the federal Parliament was slow and cautious in using its new power. Over the years, Indigenous hopes faded that the referendum result would lead to larger reforms such as the negotiation of a treaty. In time, a different concern emerged, that the races power might actually be used to discriminate against Aboriginal people, something that few foresaw when they voted Yes in 1967. By the turn of the new century, this fear became part of a new journey initiated by Aboriginal and Torres Strait Islander peoples to seek reform of the Constitution to repair the defects of 1967 and to build a stronger foundation for working with government and the broader Australian community.

After the 1967 referendum

There was much anticipation among campaigners, such as Faith Bandler, that the 1967 referendum would herald a new era of law and policy making in Aboriginal affairs. Bandler said the victory 'now gave the federal government a constituted right to create laws that would support the endeavours of Aborigines or Islanders'.[1]

In the aftermath of the poll, incremental developments occurred at a federal level under the Holt and McMahon governments, including the appointment of William Wentworth as Australia's first Minister for Aboriginal Affairs and the creation of the Council for Aboriginal Affairs. Parliament also used its new power to support state programs and grants to Aboriginal communities and organisations. This included a new fund to encourage Indigenous businesses in 1968 and an Aboriginal study grant scheme to assist Indigenous students to stay at school in 1969. Aboriginal legal and medical services were also established. However, many people were frustrated by the cautious approach taken by the Commonwealth, and its ongoing deference to the states. Aboriginal and Torres Strait Islander peoples noticed that, despite the referendum, 'discrimination did not end overnight' in their lives.[2]

Nevertheless, the referendum animated much political advocacy in the community. It gave new life to Aboriginal activism as people continued to struggle for land rights and self-determination with renewed vigour. Some of this was not a result of the referendum, but had its genesis in the earliest forms of resistance, including the political movement for sovereignty that 'had begun at the time a colony was first established in Sydney [and] shared a heart with freedom fighters like Pemulwuy'.[3]

Many people were motivated by the Gurindji in the Northern Territory. In 1966, led by Vincent Lingiari, 200 Aboriginal workers went on strike and walked off the Wave Hill cattle station demanding equal pay and land rights.

Their action still resonates today, and in the early 1990s was celebrated in the song written by Kev Carmody and Paul Kelly entitled 'From Little Things Big Things Grow'.

The struggle of the Gurindji people inspired the Federal Council for the Advancement of Aborigines and Torres Strait Islanders, which had led the 1967 referendum campaign. It adopted a new community-driven agenda based upon land rights and equal wages. At its annual conference in 1968, the organisation presented this new agenda, stressing that the Crown since 1788 had never offered to make treaties and that Aboriginal people had never been given the opportunity to regain lands that were lost. As Joe McGinness, a Kungarakan man and President of the body, told the conference, 'You can't have a people without land'.[4] Non-Indigenous campaigner Jack Horner – a veteran of the referendum campaign – likewise said: 'No issue united the Aboriginal people so much, and so openly, as that of land rights. They could see it as both an economic base for future independence and a glimmer of hope that they might run their communal affairs without political interference'.[5]

These aspirations for economic development and political power were often driven by stories of autonomy and land rights from overseas. When the National Aborigines Day

Observance Committee invited Aboriginal leaders from Canada, the United States and New Zealand to Australia in 1968, the visit drew media scrutiny because of the stark contrast between the treaties negotiated in those other nations and the ongoing struggle for land rights at home.

In 1971, Aboriginal demands for land rights took a dramatic turn when the Yolngu people sought an injunction in the Supreme Court of the Northern Territory against mining company Nabalco and the Commonwealth to stop mining at Gove. Later that year, Justice Richard Blackburn rejected their claim to land rights. He found that their customary land laws were not supported by the Australian legal system, leaving the Yolngu 'deeply shocked'.[6] It was little consolation that Justice Blackburn observed that 'the evidence shows a subtle and elaborate system highly adapted to the country ... if ever a system could be called "a government of laws, and not of men", it is that shown in the evidence before me'.[7] As far as the Yolngu were concerned, '[t]he Australian law has said that the land is not ours. This is not so. It might be right legally but ... morally it's wrong. The law must be changed'.[8]

The Gove decision intensified Aboriginal demands for land rights. In the twilight of a 23-year-long conservative rule, Prime Minister McMahon, in an Australia Day speech in 1972, rejected their claims. Instead, 50-year pastoral leases were offered to those groups who 'could make reasonable economic use of the land'.[9] This rejection of land rights was viewed by many Aboriginal people as a clear message: they were 'effectively aliens in their own land'.[10] The government's answer activated a powerful political reaction from a group of Aboriginal activists, who formed an Aboriginal Tent Embassy opposite what is now Old Parliament House in Canberra. Their protest continues to the present day, and at the time raised public and political consciousness for land rights. It was also aimed at influencing the Labor Opposition led by Gough Whitlam. The message was clear: Aboriginal and Torres Strait Islander peoples were frustrated by the lack of meaningful change in their lives as a result of the 1967 referendum.

The election of the Whitlam government in 1972 ushered in a new era of Indigenous law and policy. The government adopted the principle of self-determination – the right of people to freely determine their political, economic and cultural destiny – as underpinning its policy in Indigenous affairs. In its short time in office, the government established the first Department of Aboriginal Affairs and many other initiatives aimed at improving the plight of Aboriginal and Torres Strait Islander peoples.

Whitlam also ratified the *International Convention on the Elimination of All Forms of Racial Discrimination*, which the federal Parliament then enacted into Australian law via the *Racial Discrimination Act 1975*. This Act was to become a powerful tool for Aboriginal and other peoples in the fight against racism and to preserve native title rights.

Whitlam set up a royal commission headed by Justice Edward Woodward in 1973 to examine ways to recognise Aboriginal land rights. In response to its recommendations for broad-ranging recognition of such rights in the Northern Territory, Whitlam handed back the title deeds to Lingiari. While pouring the red Daguragu soil into the hands of Lingiari, Whitlam declared:

> Vincent Lingiari, I solemnly hand to you these deeds
> as proof in Australian law that these lands belong to
> the Gurindji people, and I put into your hands part
> of the earth itself as a sign that this land will be the
> possession of you and your children forever.[11]

The Bill for land rights in the Northern Territory had
been introduced into Parliament, but lapsed following the
dismissal of the Whitlam government on 11 November
1975. It was passed as the *Aboriginal Land Rights (Northern
Territory) Act 1976* after the Fraser government took
office.

In 1977, the Fraser government moved to create a new
representative body for Aboriginal and Torres Strait Islander
peoples called the National Aboriginal Conference (NAC).
The NAC, like its predecessor the Federal Council for the
Advancement of Aborigines and Torres Strait Islanders,
adopted an agenda that reflected the aspirations of the Indigenous community: land rights and a treaty.

Treaty and land rights

A recurring theme of Aboriginal advocacy from the years
after British settlement has been a desire for a treaty
between the state and Indigenous peoples. In 1835, John
Batman had negotiated a treaty with the Aboriginal people
of Port Phillip District in Victoria, although the treaty was
disregarded by the Victorian government. Historian Henry
Reynolds also tells the story of GA Robinson negotiating
an 'oral treaty' with Aboriginal people in Tasmania. These

aside, no treaties were negotiated between Indigenous peoples and the state at the time of colonisation. By contrast, the British made treaties with Indigenous peoples in other places, such as the Treaty of Waitangi in New Zealand and the many treaties reached in Canada and the United States.

A treaty has been viewed as a way of reaching a broad settlement between Indigenous and non-Indigenous Australians to resolve differences and enable Aboriginal people to more fully participate in the nation's political and economic systems. It could also resolve 'unfinished business', such as land rights. The idea has attracted support not only from Aboriginal people, but also the broader Australian community. Around the time the NAC was established, a coalition of non-Indigenous Australians was formed to support the negotiation of a treaty. The members of the Aboriginal Treaty Committee included prominent Australians, such as renowned anthropologist and public servant Nugget Coombs and poet Judith Wright.

In 1979, the NAC led nationwide consultations with Aboriginal and Torres Strait Islander communities on a treaty. Following this, the NAC formally announced its call for a Treaty of Commitment to be negotiated between Aboriginal people and the Commonwealth. This coincided with a decision by Justice Harry Gibbs of the High Court rejecting a claim to Aboriginal sovereignty by Wiradjuri man Paul Coe. Coe unsuccessfully argued that Captain Cook, Arthur Phillip and British settlement 'wrongfully treated the continent now known as Australia as terra nullius whereas it was occupied by the sovereign Aboriginal nation', and that 'the Aboriginal people … were entitled not to be dispossessed ... without bilateral treaty, lawful compensation and/or lawful international intervention'.[12]

The Fraser government replied to the NAC's call for a treaty by committing to future discussions. Following feedback from the Minister for Aboriginal Affairs, Fred Chaney, about the potential for the word 'treaty' to alienate ordinary Australians, the NAC resolved to replace the word 'treaty' with Makarrata, a Yolngu word meaning 'things are all right again after a conflict' or 'coming together after a struggle'.[13] The NAC then travelled around Australia to speak with Indigenous peoples about a treaty. Its interim report reflected concerns about sovereignty, the recognition of customary laws and land rights. It also suggested measures to increase Indigenous participation in Australian political life, including the reservation of seats in federal and state parliaments and local government bodies. Other proposals included the repatriation of human remains and the teaching of Aboriginal culture in schools. In early 1981, the Fraser government and the NAC exchanged letters about a Makarrata, in which the former encouraged the NAC to commence negotiations with the states and territories.

One of the final acts of the Fraser government was to constitute a Senate Standing Committee on Legal and Constitutional Affairs to examine the feasibility of securing a compact or Makarrata between the Commonwealth and Aboriginal peoples. Its 1983 report, *Two Hundred Years Later ...*, recommended that the government consider a treaty in consultation with Aboriginal people. As to the preferred method of implementation, the Committee recommended the insertion into the Constitution of a provision 'which would confer a broad power on the Commonwealth to enter into a compact with representatives of the Aboriginal people'.[14]

The NAC's campaign for a treaty was hampered by many factors, including a lack of funding, tension in the Indigenous community over the logistics of negotiating a treaty, and a dispute with the non-Indigenous Aboriginal Treaty Committee. The final straw came with the election of Prime Minister Bob Hawke in 1983. Treaty advocacy petered out as the NAC was abolished by the incoming government, which instead proposed to realise another aspect of the Aboriginal political agenda, a national Aboriginal land rights framework.

Hawke was elected at a time when Australia was turning its attention to the upcoming bicentenary of British settlement in 1988. In preparation, the government established a commission to undertake a review of the Australian Constitution. The members of the Commission included some of Australia's most distinguished politicians and jurists, such as Sir Maurice Byers, Enid Campbell, Sir Rupert Hamer, Gough Whitlam and Leslie Zines.

The final report of the Constitutional Commission was delivered in 1988 and contained several recommendations relating to Aboriginal and Torres Strait Islander peoples. These included the deletion of section 25 of the Constitution, arguing that it was 'no longer appropriate to include in the Constitution a provision which contemplates the disqualification of members of a race from voting'.[15] In addition, the report raised concerns about the races power as amended in the 1967 referendum. The Commission noted that the wording of the section permits the Parliament to pass both 'special and discriminating laws'. It recommended deleting the power because:

> Australia has joined the many nations which have
> rejected race as a legitimate criterion on which
> legislation can be based. The attitudes now officially
> adopted to discrimination on the basis of race are
> in striking contrast to those which motivated the
> Framers of the Constitution. It is appropriate that the
> change in attitude be reflected.[16]

The Commission recommended that the races power be replaced with a new power authorising the Parliament to make laws with respect to 'Aborigines and Torres Strait Islanders'. It also proposed the insertion of a clause that would prevent this and other powers being used to discriminate against any person on the basis of their race.

A treaty was also on the Commission's agenda. The body looked at the 1983 Senate Committee's idea of a federal power to enter into such agreements. The Commission recommended that such a clause be inserted into the Constitution, but that this not be open to use until a treaty had been negotiated and concluded. While the Commission recommended against a treaty at that time, it commented:

> There is no doubt that the Commonwealth has
> sufficient constitutional powers to take appropriate
> action to assist in the promotion of reconciliation with
> Aboriginal and Torres Strait Island citizens and to
> recognise their special place in the Commonwealth
> of Australia. Whether an agreement, or a number of

agreements, is an appropriate way of working to that objective has yet to be determined.[17]

As the country celebrated the bicentenary, so too did the Indigenous community commemorate the dispossession of their lands. Aboriginal people declared a 'Year of Mourning' and activists penned the slogan 'White Australia has a Black History'. On 19 January 1988, the *Sydney Morning Herald* observed that 'scarcely a day of the Bicentenary has passed when issues involving Aborigines and their "Year of Mourning" protests have not featured prominently'.[18] On 26 January 1988, when over two million Australians gathered to celebrate the bicentenary, more than 40 000 people, including Indigenous people from across the country and non-Indigenous supporters, staged what was the largest march in Sydney since the Vietnam War. Historians Peter Cochrane and David Goodman wrote:

> From the beginning, the Bicentenary has been contested ground ... The most profound challenge to the official construction of the event to be celebrated has come from Aboriginal groups. Perhaps not since the mid-nineteenth century has the basic question of [the] right to occupy the continent been posed with such clarity, and received such mainstream attention.[19]

On 12 June that year, a special meeting of Aboriginal people took place in Barunga, Northern Territory. In the years leading up to the bicentenary, the leaders of the major Aboriginal land councils, including Galarrwuy Yunupingu, Wenten Rubuntja and Patrick Dodson and other Aboriginal leaders, had worked on a petition of political claims. The Barunga Statement was inspired by the Yirrkala Bark Petitions sent to the Parliament in 1963 objecting to mining on Yolngu country. The Barunga demands were typed and affixed to a bark painting depicting many of the Northern Territory clans, including Yolngu and the Central Desert. The Statement called for recognition of Aboriginal rights and for the federal Parliament to pass laws providing for:

- A national elected Aboriginal and Islander organisation to oversee Aboriginal and Islander affairs;
- A national system of land rights;
- A police and justice system which recognises our customary laws and frees us from discrimination and any activity which may threaten our identity or security, interfere with our freedom of expression or association, or otherwise prevent our full enjoyment and exercise of universally recognised human rights and fundamental freedoms.[20]

The Statement also called upon the Commonwealth to 'negotiate with us a Treaty recognising our prior ownership, continued occupation and sovereignty and affirming our human rights and freedom'.[21]

The Statement was presented personally to the Prime Minister in 1988. In reply, Hawke declared that there would be a treaty within the life of the current Parliament, saying:

> There shall be a treaty negotiated between the
> Aboriginal people and the Government on behalf of
> all the people of Australia … these processes should

start before the end of this year and ... we would
expect and hope and work for the conclusion of such a
treaty before the end of the life of this Parliament.[22]

Hawke delivered on only one of the demands presented to him by the Barunga Statement: a new elected representative body. Following an extensive consultation period that included 500 meetings with 14 500 people (including 6000 personal discussions between Minister Gerry Hand and Aboriginal and Torres Strait Islander people), the federal Parliament created an independent statutory body called the Aboriginal and Torres Strait Islander Commission (ATSIC) in 1989.

By the time he was deposed as Prime Minister by Paul Keating, Hawke had neither negotiated a treaty nor had Parliament legislated for national land rights. Days after abandoning a uniform national land rights package, the Prime Minister told the National Press Club that 'Australians as a whole weren't as compassionate as they were in 1967, when the Federal Government was given power over Aboriginal affairs'.[23] In an interview on ABC Television's *Four Corners*, Patrick Dodson said that 'Aboriginal people view the spirit of the '67 Referendum going down the drain'.[24]

Reflecting the frustrations of the time, the song 'Treaty' was written by Yothu Yindi in collaboration with Paul Kelly and Midnight Oil. The song captured the sense of anticipation at the commitment that there would be a treaty and disappointment at the failure to honour it.[25]

Hawke's failure to deliver on the issues most important to Aboriginal and Torres Strait Islander peoples signalled the next phase on the journey to constitutional reform: reconciliation. Reconciliation was conceived by Hawke as a political solution to broken promises and the perennial demands for land rights and a treaty.

Reconciliation

Australia's 'decade of reconciliation' commenced in 1991, when the federal Parliament enacted a law establishing the Council for Aboriginal Reconciliation. The *Council for Aboriginal Reconciliation Act 1991* acknowledged that there had been 'no formal process of reconciliation between Aborigines and Torres Strait Islanders and other Australians'.[26] The reaction was mixed. Many Indigenous people were dismayed at the slide from a treaty to what they saw as 'a somewhat desultory reconciliation process'.[27] This included Aboriginal poet Kevin Gilbert, who felt that 'the reconciliation process can achieve nothing because it does not at the end of the day promise justice'.[28]

Even so, the preamble to the Act contained some weighty notions, including that 'Australia was occupied by Aborigines and Torres Strait Islanders who had settled for thousands of years, before British settlement at Sydney Cove on 26 January 1788', and that 'many Aborigines and Torres Strait Islanders suffered dispossession and dispersal from their traditional lands by the British Crown'.[29] In addition, the Council included a broad membership from across the community. Its co-chairs were Evelyn Scott, a Torres Strait Islander, and scientist Sir Gustav Nossal.

The purpose of the Council was to lead a national

process of reconciliation leading up to the Centenary of
Federation in 2001. The three goals of Council were to create
formal documents of reconciliation, develop partnerships
based upon reconciliation and build a people's movement
for reconciliation. Each required the Council to lead a
nationwide consultative process to seek the views of all Australians and raise public awareness of reconciliation. The
reconciliation movement, led by the Council, grew during
the 1990s and was boosted by gestures such as the 1992
Redfern Speech delivered by Prime Minister Paul Keating.
He acknowledged the history of Australia and the wrongs
committed against Aboriginal people by the colonisers:

> It was we who did the dispossessing.
>
> We took the traditional lands and smashed
> the traditional way of life.
>
> We brought the diseases and the alcohol.
> We committed the murders.
>
> We took the children from their mothers …
>
> We failed to ask – how would I feel if this were
> done to me?[30]

That same year, the High Court of Australia handed down
its decision in *Mabo*.[31] It was the culmination of a ten-year
legal struggle by the Meriam people seeking rights to the use
and enjoyment of their traditional lands in the Torres Strait.
The action had been commenced by five Murray Islanders,

including Eddie Mabo. The question asked by the Murray Islanders was whether, on acquiring sovereignty, the Crown had gained complete ownership of the land, or whether it was burdened by any prior Aboriginal title. The Court rejected the idea that Australia was *terra nullius*, or no man's land, at the time of British settlement. It held as a result that the pre-existing native title rights of Indigenous peoples continued to exist.

Following the *Mabo* decision, Keating negotiated a three-part response to address the dispossession of Aboriginal and Torres Strait Islander peoples. These were the *Native Title Act 1993*, the Indigenous Land Corporation, and a Social Justice Package to compensate Indigenous peoples who had been dispossessed and unable to claim native title.

An ATSIC committee led by Charles Perkins and the Human Rights and Equal Opportunity Commission's Aboriginal and Torres Strait Islander Social Justice Commissioner Mick Dodson led consultations with the Aboriginal and Torres Strait Islander community on an appropriate social justice response to the High Court's landmark decision in *Mabo*. The ATSIC committee submitted to the Prime Minister a report entitled 'Recognition, Rights and Reform', which reaffirmed community aspirations to constitutional recognition in light of *Mabo*: '[T]he Commonwealth Government should note that the national consultation process in relation to the Social Justice Package showed overwhelming support for the reform of the Constitution especially in relation to recognition of Indigenous peoples'.

The Social Justice Package reforms included suggestions that the federal Parliament use the power it gained in the 1967 referendum to initiate major institutional and structural changes. These included regional self-government and regional agreements, and the negotiation of a treaty or comparable document addressing the issue of compensation.

At this point, the process floundered. Keating lost the 1996 election to the Liberal–National Coalition led by John Howard. The new government abandoned the Social Justice Package, meaning that this third pillar of the *Mabo* response was never delivered.

The Howard era

There were more setbacks to come during the 1990s. In particular, two High Court decisions led to a deep divide between Aboriginal people and the government, and an often bitter political debate. The first decision in *Wik* related to native title, the second in the *Hindmarsh Island Bridge Case* to the unintended consequences of the 1967 referendum.

On 23 December 1996, the High Court handed down the *Wik* decision, which held that pastoral leases do not necessarily extinguish native title. The Howard government responded with the *Native Title Amendment Act 1998*. It implemented a 'ten point plan' that, in the words of Deputy Prime Minister Tim Fischer, sought to pour 'bucket-loads of extinguishment'[32] on the native title rights of Indigenous Australians. To wind back these native title rights, the *Native Title Amendment Act 1998* suspended the operation of the *Racial Discrimination Act*. This cleared the way for the law to adversely discriminate against Aboriginal native title claimants by reducing their rights in favour of the rights of others.

During the negotiations for the *Wik* amendments, another challenge to reconciliation emerged. On 26 May 1997, the Human Rights and Equal Opportunity Commission tabled the *Bringing Them Home* report. Initiated during the Keating government, the Inquiry examined the former practice of separating Aboriginal and Torres Strait Islander children from their families. One of the chief recommendations was an apology to those Stolen Generations. However, Prime Minister Howard opposed an apology because he believed that Australians 'should not be required to accept guilt and blame for past actions and policies over which they had no control'.[33] He said that, 'if I have not been part of any wrongdoing and if I'm not part of a generation that's been part of that wrongdoing, I've always had a difficulty in assuming responsibility for the claimed wrongdoings of earlier generations, particularly when those acts were sanctioned by the law of the country'.[34]

The Prime Minister's position was a source of tension between him and Indigenous peoples throughout his time in government. During Howard's speech to the Australian Reconciliation Convention in 1997, many attendees stood up and turned their backs in protest that he refused to say sorry to the Stolen Generations. It was not until his second term of office that on 26 August 1999 he introduced a Motion of Reconciliation into Parliament, which had been developed in consultation with Aboriginal Senator Aden Ridgeway, a member of the Democrats. The Motion expressed its 'deep and sincere regret that Indigenous Australians suffered injustices under the practices of past generations, and for the hurt and trauma that many Indigenous people continue to feel as a consequence of those practices'.[35] The Motion was criticised by Aboriginal and Torres Strait Islander peoples because of the Prime Minister's insistence on using the word 'regret' instead of 'sorry'. The use of the former word was regarded as being insincere.

The second High Court decision came in 1998. One of the Howard government's first acts when it came to power in 1996 had been to shepherd legislation through Parliament, relying on the races power, to prevent the Ngarrindjeri Aboriginal women in South Australia from invoking the *Aboriginal and Torres Strait Islander Heritage Protection Act 1984* to stop the construction of a bridge over an area where they engaged in secret women's business. The *Hindmarsh Island Bridge Act 1997* restricted the operation of the *Heritage Protection Act* so that it applied everywhere in Australia except for the Hindmarsh Island bridge area.

This legislation was challenged by the Ngarrindjeri women in the High Court on the basis that the races power – as amended in 1967 – cannot be used in an adverse or detrimental manner by the Commonwealth. The Commonwealth responded by arguing that there are no limits on the power so long as the law imposed a consequence based on race.

Effectively, the Commonwealth was arguing that it could use the races power to pass discriminatory laws. Lest there was any doubt about this, the Commonwealth's lawyer, Solicitor General Gavan Griffith, said to the High Court that the races power 'is infected, the power is infused with a power of adverse operation'. He also acknowledged its 'direct racist content', in the sense of 'a capacity for adverse operation'. This prompted the following exchange between Justice Michael Kirby and Griffith:

JUSTICE KIRBY: Can I just get clear in my mind, is the Commonwealth's submission that it is entirely and exclusively for the Parliament to determine the matter upon which special laws are deemed necessary or whatever the words say or is there a point at which there is a justiciable question for the Court? I mean, it seems unthinkable that a law such as the Nazi race laws could be enacted under the race power and that this Court could do nothing about it.

MR GRIFFITH: Your Honour, if there was a reason why the Court could do something about it, a Nazi law, it would, in our submission, be for a reason external to the races power. It would be for some wider overarching reason.[36]

On 1 April 1998, the High Court handed down its decision upholding the *Hindmarsh Island Bridge Act*, thereby rejecting the claims of the Ngarrindjeri women. The judgments left open the possibility that the Commonwealth can use the races power to impose racially discriminatory laws upon Aboriginal people.

This decision was a turning point in post-1967 Aboriginal advocacy. The prospect that the federal Parliament had gained a power to discriminate against Aboriginal people was alarming. This caught the attention of the United Nations committee tasked to monitor domestic implementation of the treaty upon which the *Racial Discrimination Act* was based. The Committee on the Elimination of Racial Discrimination was so disturbed by these developments that it placed Australia on its early warning urgent action list, the first Western country to be so named.

By 1998, although Aboriginal people continued to call for the negotiation of a treaty, the debate had shifted considerably. The emergence of a national conversation about Australia becoming a republic during Keating's time as Prime Minister led people to ask how Indigenous peoples might be acknowledged if Australia made that shift. During his first term, Howard convened a ten-day Constitutional Convention at Old Parliament House in Canberra in February 1998 to consider whether Australia should become a republic, and to debate the model.

The Convention comprised 152 delegates, half of whom were elected and half who were parliamentary representatives and government appointees. One issue at the Convention was whether the move to a republic should also bring with it a new preamble, or opening words, to the Constitution. Chairman of the Australian Republican Movement Malcolm Turnbull argued that if a preamble 'is to remain a statement of history, then it should pay appropriate regard and respect to Aboriginal history'.[37] The Convention recommended that a new preamble to the Constitution provide explicit 'acknowledgement of the original occupancy and custodianship of Australia by Aboriginal peoples and Torres Strait Islanders', and 'recognition that Aboriginal people and Torres Strait Islanders have continuing rights by virtue of their status as Australia's indigenous peoples'.[38]

The focus on a preamble reflected a significant shift in thinking. It involved a move away from considering more substantial forms of recognition, such as giving legal force to rights to land, to symbolic recognition in the Constitution. At the time, Indigenous peoples were reassured by the fact that the Council for Aboriginal Reconciliation was continuing its work towards developing a roadmap for reconciliation that could include such substantive measures. Nevertheless, the Council cautioned that a new preamble carried dangers because it might 'be seen as an easy symbolic step which would be all that was needed to address constitutional issues for Indigenous peoples'.[39]

Prime Minister Howard took the lead in drafting the new preamble. In March 1999, he engaged poet Les Murray to co-write the text. The Howard–Murray preamble read:

> With hope in God, the Commonwealth of Australia is constituted by the equal sovereignty of all its citizens.
>
> The Australian nation is woven together of people from many ancestries and arrivals.
>
> Our vast island continent has helped to shape the destiny of our Commonwealth and the spirit of its people.
>
> Since time immemorial our land has been inhabited by Aborigines and Torres Strait Islanders, who are honoured for their ancient and continuing cultures.
>
> In every generation immigrants have brought great enrichment to our nation's life.

Australians are free to be proud of their country and
heritage, free to realise themselves as individuals, and
free to pursue their hopes and ideals.

We value excellence as well as fairness, independence
as dearly as mateship.

Australia's democratic and federal system of
government exists under law to preserve and protect
all Australians in an equal dignity which may never
be infringed by prejudice or fashion or ideology nor
invoked against achievement.

In this spirit we, the Australian people, commit
ourselves to this Constitution.[40]

This version was widely ridiculed, in part because of
its reference to 'mateship'. The reference to Aboriginal
and Torres Strait Islander peoples was also panned by
Indigenous leaders, including Michael Mansell, Peter Yu,
Lowitja O'Donoghue and Gatjil Djerrkura. They regarded
it as failing to go beyond recognition of prior occupation
and criticised its failure to use the word 'custodianship'
suggested by the Constitutional Convention.

Murray resigned from the process because he felt
that his language was being interfered with, stating that,
'[t]he preamble has now been compromised away to
mush, compromised so much it doesn't matter anymore.
I'm not saying that out of peevishness. It went into the
political compromise machine and came out mush'.[41] At

this point, the Australian Labor Party and the Australian Republic Movement argued for the preamble proposal to be abandoned entirely because they thought it risked diverting attention away from the move to a republic.

The Prime Minister then engaged Democrats Senator Aden Ridgeway to assist him to revise the wording. According to Howard, 'the fact that the two of us have come together ... symbolises the value of the preamble as a uniting element in constitutional debate in Australia'.[42] The collaboration led to a new draft that was passed by Parliament and then, along with the proposal for a republic, put to the Australian people at a referendum in 1999. This final version read:

> With hope in God, the Commonwealth of Australia is constituted as a democracy with a federal system of government to serve the common good.
>
> We the Australian people commit ourselves to this Constitution:
>
> proud that our national unity has been forged by Australians from many ancestries;
>
> never forgetting the sacrifices of all who defended our country and our liberty in time of war;
>
> upholding freedom, tolerance, individual dignity and the rule of law;

honouring Aborigines and Torres Strait Islanders, the nation's first people, for their deep kinship with their lands and for their ancient and continuing cultures which enrich the life of our country;

recognising the nation building contribution of generations of immigrants;

mindful of our responsibility to protect our unique natural environment;

supportive of achievement as well as equality of opportunity for all;

and valuing independence as dearly as the national spirit which binds us together in both adversity and success.[43]

The line acknowledging Aboriginal and Torres Strait Islander peoples was again criticised by Indigenous leaders. It did not adopt the word 'custodianship', which had been put forward by the Constitutional Convention as best describing the Aboriginal connection to land. Rather, the word 'kinship' was used to describe this relationship. For many leaders, 'kinship' did not easily apply to the connection between a person and a place or thing. ATSIC Chairman Gatjil Djerrkura said 'the term "kinship" in my view, is a word that describes personal relationship, people's relationship. It doesn't reflect a relationship to the land. Custodianship, yes'.[44]

Senator Ridgeway replied to critics by saying that their objections were 'too legal or too anthropological'. He said he had grappled with how to capture traditional ownership, stewardship and custodianship in a single word and 'I think that kinship achieves that'.[45] Peter Yu, head of the Kimberley Land Council, disagreed, arguing: '[The preamble] doesn't reflect the fundamental truth ... that we are the original occupiers and owners of this country ... and continue to have existing rights'.[46] More generally, such concerns reflected a lack of consultation with Aboriginal and Torres Strait Islander leaders. When the Prime Minister was asked if he had consulted other Indigenous leaders, he replied that he had not.

Together, Howard and Ridgeway insisted that their preamble would advance the cause of reconciliation because the text of the Constitution otherwise contained no reference to Aboriginal and Torres Strait Islander peoples. Nonetheless, the preamble was soundly rejected by Australian voters. The referendum held on 6 November 1999 saw the preamble rejected by every state and territory, and nationally it attracted a No vote of 60.7 per cent (a significantly worse result than that for the republic, which was also defeated). The rejection was pronounced in electorates with Aboriginal and Torres Strait Islander populations.

On celebrating the preamble's failure, poet Murray joked that 'the Australian people had mercifully taken it out the back and shot it'.[47] For Djerrkura, the preamble 'did not promote reconciliation or advance our aspirations. I welcome its resounding defeat'. In addition he said the process of drafting the preamble lacked 'proper consultation' with Indigenous people.[48]

A feature of the failed preamble was the inclusion of a clause recommended by the Constitutional Convention that provided that the preamble could have no legal effect. This was expressed in proposed clause 125A, which provided that 'the preamble to this Constitution has no legal force and shall not be considered in interpreting this Constitution or the law in force in the Commonwealth or any part of the Commonwealth'.[49] This clause was designed to placate those who feared that the High Court might use a new preamble to imply new rights from the Constitution, such as to support the interests of Aboriginal people. Others saw the clause as suggesting insincerity, or as being excessive and alarmist, not least because the High Court has historically treated the existing preamble in the Constitution 'with a mix of indifference and reticence'.[50]

The results of reconciliation

Following the failed referendum, the nation moved towards the final chapter of the reconciliation era. A decade after its creation, the Council for Aboriginal Reconciliation finally delivered its *Roadmap for Reconciliation*. This contained the National Strategy for Recognising Aboriginal and Torres Strait Islander Peoples' Rights, which recommended that a referendum be held to change the Constitution to:

- recognise Aboriginal and Torres Strait Islander peoples as the first peoples of Australia in a new preamble to the Constitution; and

- remove section 25 of the Constitution and introduce
  a new section making it unlawful to adversely
  discriminate against any people on the grounds of
  race.[51]

The Council's recommendations, addressed to Prime
Minister Howard, also included that 'the Commonwealth
Parliament enact legislation … to put in place a process
which will unite all Australians by way of an agreement,
or treaty, through which unresolved issues of reconciliation
can be resolved'.[52] By these recommendations, the Council
reinforced Aboriginal and Torres Strait Islander aspirations
for a treaty and echoed the Constitutional Commission's
call for a racial non-discrimination clause.

On 27 May 2000, at an event called Corroboree 2000,
the Council presented the *Australian Declaration towards
Reconciliation* and the *Roadmap for Reconciliation* to the
Australian people and the Prime Minister. The reconciliation documents arrived at the Man O' War steps outside the
Sydney Opera House aboard the vessel *Tribal Warrior*. The
documents were met with a smoking ceremony before being
carried in a procession into the Opera House. Governor-
General Sir William Deane told the audience:

> It's wrong to see those past injustices as belonging, as
> it were, to another country … they have been absorbed
> into the present and the future of contemporary
> Indigenous Australians and of the nation of which
> they form such an important part. They – and the land
> that was taken – are our country.[53]

The next day, the Council delivered spectacularly on its other goal to 'build a people's movement toward reconciliation',[54] when one million people walked in capital cities and towns in support of reconciliation. This gesture, known as the Bridge Walks, reflected the years that the Council had spent raising awareness of the importance of reconciliation to the future of the nation. The Sydney leg of the Bridge Walks saw 300 000 people walk across the Sydney Harbour Bridge. It was reported that the Sydney march started just after 8 am, 'behind the golf buggies carrying Indigenous elders from across Australia'. According to one newspaper report, some 25 000 Sydneysiders walked in the first timeslot, and 'many of them walked in silence. Some cried ... It was an extraordinary display of harmony and togetherness'.[55]

While the Council's efforts were a political response to Hawke's broken promises, the Bridge Walks demonstrated what could be achieved in raising community consciousness through leadership and an orchestrated campaign. The success of the Bridge Walks also suggested that political sentiment was out of touch with the public's desire to reconcile with Australia's first peoples. The day after the Bridge Walks, Prime Minister Howard, who had refused to participate in the walks, dismissed the Council's recommendation for a treaty. He said that, 'a nation ... does not make a treaty with itself'.[56]

Despite Howard's opposition to a treaty, on 8 November 2000, the *Sydney Morning Herald* reported an increase in the number of Australians who supported this outcome. The Herald–ACNielsen poll found 53 per cent of Australians were in favour of a treaty, 'with those opposed dropping 6 per cent to 34 per cent over the previous poll in June'.[57]

The poll also found that support for reconciliation had risen from 74 per cent to 78 per cent.

The work towards a treaty passed over to the leadership of ATSIC, which picked up where the Council and NAC had left off. ATSIC hoped to build upon the final report of the Council for Aboriginal Reconciliation, which had called on governments to:

> recognise that this land and its waters were settled as colonies without treaty or consent, and that to advance reconciliation it would be most desirable if there were agreements or treaties, and to negotiate a process through which this might be achieved that protects the political, legal, cultural and economic position of Aboriginal and Torres Strait Islander peoples.[58]

ATSIC's intent was not to negotiate a treaty, but to provide information and to facilitate a process that would allow the Indigenous community to negotiate a treaty with the state. However, this collided with the Prime Minister's agenda of 'practical reconciliation'.

Howard created an artificial dichotomy between practical and symbolic reconciliation. He characterised the issues to be focused on as socio-economic disadvantage such as housing, education, employment and health, as opposed to symbolism, which he equated with substantive rights. He reinforced his long-held rejection of symbolic reconciliation when, in the wake of the failed 1999 referendum, he said that reconciliation in the form of Indigenous rights, a treaty, Stolen Generations and deaths in custody had failed.

One consequence of this was the demise of ATSIC itself. With the support of the Australian Labor Party, Parliament passed a law in 2004 that abolished the body. ATSIC Commissioner Steve Gordon suggested that this was designed to stop the treaty process. It has also since been argued that the abolition of ATSIC was to prevent regional autonomy plans devised by ATSIC to enhance the economic development of Indigenous communities.

4

THE JOURNEY TO RECOGNITION

The failure of the 1999 referendum did not end attempts to achieve constitutional recognition of Aboriginal and Torres Strait Islander peoples by way of a preamble or other words. The push for this continued, although initially only in the states. Change is easier to achieve at this level as the states can usually amend their constitutions by way of an ordinary Act of Parliament.

Victoria was the first to amend its Constitution to bring this about. It did so in 2004 by inserting the following as a new section 1A:

Recognition of Aboriginal people

(1) The Parliament acknowledges that the events described in the Preamble to this Act occurred without proper consultation, recognition or involvement of the Aboriginal people of Victoria.

(2) The Parliament recognises that Victoria's Aboriginal people, as the original custodians of the land on which the Colony of Victoria was established –

(a) have a unique status as the descendants of Australia's first people; and

(b) have a spiritual, social, cultural and economic relationship with their traditional lands and waters within Victoria; and

(c) have made a unique and irreplaceable contribution to the identity and well-being of Victoria.[1]

This section comes after the existing preamble to that Constitution, which recites things such as the creation of the self-governing colony of Victoria in 1854.

Queensland, New South Wales and South Australia followed suit.[2] However, Indigenous peoples expressed strong concern about the recognition provided, as the added words are in each case accompanied by what is known as a no-legal effect clause or a non-justiciability clause. For example, the words recognising Aboriginal people in the South Australian Constitution are accompanied by a clause stating that 'the Parliament does not intend this section to have any legal force or effect'.[3]

As with the attempt in 1999 to insert a similar clause into the Australian Constitution, the effect was to undermine Indigenous support because of a perception that this limited recognition is insincere. When the final states of Western Australia and Tasmania changed their constitutions to recognise their Indigenous populations, they did not see such a clause as being necessary. They chose instead to include unfettered words of acknowledgment.

Facing defeat at the 2007 general election, Prime Minister Howard once again expressed his support for recognising Indigenous Australians in the Constitution by way of symbolic change. He announced three days prior to the vote:

> I announce that, if re-elected, I will put to the Australian people within eighteen months a referendum to formally recognise Indigenous Australians in our Constitution – their history as the first inhabitants of our country, their unique heritage of culture and languages, and their special (though not separate) place within a reconciled, indivisible nation.

> My goal is to see a new Statement of Reconciliation incorporated into the Preamble of the Australian Constitution. If elected, I would commit immediately to working in consultation with Indigenous leaders and others on this task ...

> I would aim to introduce a [B]ill that would include the Preamble Statement into Parliament within the first 100 days of a new government.

> A future referendum question would stand alone. It would not be blurred or cluttered by other constitutional considerations. I would seek to enlist wide community support for a 'Yes' vote. I would hope and aim to secure the sort of overwhelming vote achieved 40 years ago at the 1967 referendum.

If approached in the right spirit, I believe this is both realistic and achievable.[4]

Given the timing, the proposal was met with scepticism, not least because Howard confirmed that, once again, he had consulted only one Aboriginal leader, in this case Noel Pearson. Nevertheless, his speech was an olive branch of sorts given the difficult relationship he had had with Indigenous peoples during his term of office.

An Apology and the Expert Panel

One of the first acts of newly elected Prime Minister Kevin Rudd was to issue an Apology to Australia's Stolen Generations. Rudd's speech on 13 February 2008 distinguished itself from Howard's Motion of Reconciliation by using the word 'sorry':

> For the pain, suffering and hurt of these Stolen Generations, their descendants and for their families left behind, we say sorry.

> To the mothers and the fathers, the brothers and the sisters, for the breaking up of families and communities, we say sorry.

> And for the indignity and degradation thus inflicted on a proud people and a proud culture, we say sorry.[5]

This was a powerful statement by the Prime Minister on behalf of the Parliament of Australia. It was received with great emotion and joy by Aboriginal and Torres Strait Islander peoples, many of whom declared that for the first time in their lives they felt Australian. In making the apology, Rudd also touched upon the 'constitutional recognition of the first Australians',[6] saying that he wanted to maintain bipartisan support for the idea.

Constitutional recognition was back on the agenda again in April 2008 when the Prime Minister hosted the Australia 2020 Summit to generate ideas for building a modern Australia. One of the streams was 'Options for the Future of Indigenous Australia'. A key outcome of this stream was support for a new national dialogue on reconciliation and the formal legal recognition of Indigenous peoples. In particular, the final report noted the 'strong view that recognition of Aboriginal and Torres Strait Islander peoples' rights needs to be included in the body of the Constitution, not just in the Preamble'.[7]

In the 'Governance' stream of the Summit, Indigenous issues were also raised in relation to the theme of constitution, rights and responsibilities. This stream recommended as its top priority that the Constitution be amended to include a preamble that formally recognises the traditional custodians of Australian land and waters, that the Constitution be amended to remove any language that is racially discriminatory, and that a national process be conducted to consider a compact of reconciliation between Indigenous and non-Indigenous Australians.

Following the 2020 Summit, a community cabinet was held in eastern Arnhem Land on 23 July. Prime Minister

Rudd was presented with a Statement of Intent from Yolngu and Bininj leaders in which members of those communities expressed their desire for constitutional protection for traditional land and cultural rights. The communiqué was written on behalf of Yolngu and Bininj clans living in the Yirrkala, Gunyangara, Gapuwiyak, Maningrida, Galiwin'ku, Milingimbi, Ramingining and Laynhapuy homelands, constituting approximately 8000 Indigenous people in Arnhem Land. It had been developed over 18 months in meetings at Maningrida in western Arnhem Land.

The communiqué was handed to the Prime Minister by Yolngu and Bininj people, who stated they had been 'marginalised and demeaned over the past decade and [had] been denied real opportunity to have a say about [their] aspirations and futures'.[8] They argued for the preconditions for economic and community development in remote communities, including the right to be recognised as maintaining their culture and identity, and protection of their land and sea estates. They also argued for the importance of recognising their right to live on their land and practise their culture, and requested that the Australian government 'work towards constitutional recognition of our prior ownership and rights'.[9]

In accepting this communiqué, Rudd pledged his support for recognition of Indigenous peoples in the Constitution. He said that there was:

> nothing new about the fact that the national platform
> of the Australian Labor Party has said for some
> time that we've committed to the constitutional

recognition of the first Australians. That is not new; it's been around for a long time. That remains our commitment.[10]

In response, Opposition Leader Dr Brendan Nelson offered bipartisan support for an amended preamble to recognise 'the place of Indigenous people in Australian life'.[11] His comments were consistent with the Liberal Party's 2007 election platform and former Prime Minister Howard's pledge just before the federal election of that year.

At the time, it was widely reported and assumed by the media and political leaders that any constitutional recognition of Indigenous Australians would come in the form of a new preamble. However, the idea that recognition required no more than this neglected the broader aspirations of Aboriginal people, and was based on a misreading of the Yolngu/Bininj Statement of Intent. That document had, for example, also argued for recognition of land rights.

It sought substantive constitutional rights, not symbolism. After 50 years of advocacy, the goals and aspirations of Aboriginal and Torres Strait Islander peoples continued to be cherry-picked by political parties and the media. Even when Indigenous peoples have called for substantive constitutional recognition, politicians often heard 'symbolic' recognition. This has meant, too often, that constitutional reform has been understood as being synonymous with minimal change such as new opening words to the Constitution.

Due to a leadership spill in the Labor Party, Julia Gillard, rather than Rudd, led the government to the 2010 federal election. That vote resulted in a hung Parliament. Gillard was able to retain her position as Prime Minister by securing the support of Greens and Independent members. In return, she made a number of policy commitments, including holding a referendum during the life of the Parliament or at the next election on Indigenous constitutional recognition.

At the end of 2010, Prime Minister Gillard established an Expert Panel to report on possible options to give effect to Indigenous constitutional recognition and to advise on the level of support from Indigenous people and the broader community for each option. The Panel was led by Professor Patrick Dodson, former Chairman of the Council for Aboriginal Reconciliation, and Mark Leibler, former Reconciliation Australia co-chair. The Panel's membership was half Indigenous and half non-Indigenous, selected after a public nomination process. Members included representatives of each of Australia's major parties, as well as people such as Noel Pearson, Marcia Langton, Fred Chaney, and the co-chairs of the National Congress of Australia's First Peoples.

The Expert Panel was charged with leading a national consultation and engagement program to seek the views of a wide spectrum of the community, based on a discussion paper that set out ideas for reform. It travelled the length and breadth of Australia between May and October 2011, holding more than 250 meetings in 84 remote, regional and metropolitan areas. People at these meetings were asked whether the Constitution should be changed and, if so, how. The Panel also published a discussion paper, held a formal public submission process, and produced a website – all of which were aimed at capturing the views of as many people as possible.

Expert Panel's recommendations for changes to the Constitution[12]

The Panel recommends:

1. That section 25 be repealed.

2. That section 51(xxvi) be repealed.

3. That a new 'section 51A' be inserted, along the following lines:

Section 51A Recognition of Aboriginal and Torres Strait Islander peoples

Recognising that the continent and its islands now known as Australia were first occupied by Aboriginal and Torres Strait Islander peoples;

Acknowledging the continuing relationship of Aboriginal and Torres Strait Islander peoples with their traditional lands and waters;

Respecting the continuing cultures, languages and heritage of Aboriginal and Torres Strait Islander peoples;

Acknowledging the need to secure the advancement of Aboriginal and Torres Strait Islander peoples;

the Parliament shall, subject to this Constitution, have power to make laws for the peace, order and good government of the Commonwealth with respect to Aboriginal and Torres Strait Islander peoples.

The Panel further recommends that the repeal of section 51(xxvi) and the insertion of the new 'section 51A' be proposed together.

4. That a new 'section 116A' be inserted, along the following lines:

Section 116A Prohibition of racial discrimination

(1) The Commonwealth, a State or a Territory shall not discriminate on the grounds of race, colour or ethnic or national origin.

(2) Subsection (1) does not preclude the making of laws or measures for the purpose of overcoming disadvantage, ameliorating the effects of past discrimination, or protecting the cultures, languages or heritage of any group.

5. That a new 'section 127A' be inserted, along the following lines:

Section 127A Recognition of languages

(1) The national language of the Commonwealth of Australia is English.

(3) The Aboriginal and Torres Strait Islander languages are the original Australian languages, a part of our national heritage.

The Panel received over 3500 submissions from members of the public, members of Parliament, Aboriginal and Torres Strait Islander leaders, organisations and individuals, community groups, legal professionals and academics. In developing its proposals for reform, it met with Indigenous leaders across Australia and constitutional law experts. The Panel adopted four principles to guide its assessment of proposals, namely that a proposal must:

1   contribute to a more unified and reconciled nation;
2   be of benefit to and accord with the wishes of
    Aboriginal and Torres Strait Islander peoples;
3   be capable of being supported by an overwhelming
    majority of Australians from across the political and
    social spectrums; and
4   be technically and legally sound.[13]

The Panel's report, released in early 2012, identified strong community support for changing the Constitution to acknowledge Aboriginal and Torres Strait Islander peoples. As set out on pages 98–99, it recommended specific options for reform, including inserting words of recognition, removing the remaining clauses that enable discrimination on the basis of race and inserting a new clause to protect all people from racial discrimination.

Acts of recognition

The Gillard government did not respond to the Panel's report, nor did it seek to put any referendum, saying that the political environment was not consistent with maintaining bipartisan support and a referendum might fail due to low levels of community awareness.

Instead, it funded Reconciliation Australia to raise community awareness of the issue. That led to the creation of Recognise, a body funded and supervised by Reconciliation Australia that was actively involved in explaining to Australians what this issue is about, and why they should support reform. Among other things, Recognise initiated a Journey to Recognition relay around the country that by late 2014 had travelled 28 000 kilometres, passing through 188 communities and holding 238 events engaging with over 17 500 people. Recognise was active until 2017, when it was wound down.

In the absence of a referendum, the Gillard government introduced a measure into Parliament to provide an interim form of recognition of Aboriginal people. This law, the *Aboriginal and Torres Strait Islander Peoples Recognition Act 2013*, was passed with cross-party support. It incorporated recognition by stating that 'the Parliament, on behalf of the people of Australia, acknowledges the continuing relationship of Aboriginal and Torres Strait Islander peoples with their traditional lands and waters'.[14]

The Act stipulated that the Minister should conduct a review within 12 months to consider the readiness of the Australian public to support a referendum; consider proposals for constitutional change to recognise Aboriginal and Torres Strait Islander peoples, taking into account the work of the Expert Panel and Reconciliation Australia; and identify which of those proposals would be most likely to obtain the support of the Australian people.

This review was also asked to determine the level of support for amending the Constitution to recognise Aboriginal and Torres Strait Islander peoples among Indigenous peoples, the wider Australian public and the governments of the states and territories. The Australian Labor Party regarded the review as preventing any future Abbott government from letting the issue slide.

The Act was set to lapse in two years (in 2015), on the basis that it was only intended as a stopgap measure until the Constitution was changed. However, in 2015, the Constitution had still not been changed. Parliament therefore passed the *Aboriginal and Torres Strait Islander Peoples Recognition (Sunset Extension) Act 2015*, which replaced the initial two-year lapse period with a five-year period. The Act was finally repealed in 2018.

In a rare example of bipartisanship for the time, Opposition Leader Tony Abbott spoke strongly in favour of the Act and the idea of constitutional recognition in general. He said:

> Australia is a blessed country. Our climate, our land, our people, our institutions rightly make us the envy of the earth, except for one thing – we have never fully made peace with the First Australians. This is the stain on our soul that Prime Minister Keating so movingly evoked at Redfern 21 years ago. We have to acknowledge that pre-1788 this land was as Aboriginal then as it is Australian now. Until we have acknowledged that, we will be an incomplete nation and a torn people.[15]

He argued that a referendum should be held after the 2013 election, saying:

> I believe that we are equal to this task of completing our Constitution rather than changing it. The next parliament will, I trust, finish the work that this one has begun.[16]

Each of Australia's major parties at the 2013 federal election expressed strong support for recognising Aboriginal peoples in the Constitution. These commitments were, however, light on detail. No party provided a considered response to the options recommended by the Expert Panel. Abbott did, however, express scepticism about the insertion of any clause into the Constitution that might protect people from racial discrimination. He described the Panel's recommendation to this effect as being a 'one-clause Bill of Rights'.[17]

As the victor of the 2013 election, Abbott said that he wanted to be Australia's first 'Prime Minister for Aboriginal Affairs'. Consistent with this, he repeated on several occasions his support for recognising Aboriginal peoples in the Constitution. For example, he said in his 2014 Australia Day address:

> We will also begin a national conversation about amending our Constitution to recognise Aboriginal peoples as the first Australians. This should be another unifying moment in the history of our country.[18]

He also said that his government would release a timetable and concrete proposal for achieving constitutional recognition. The Prime Minister's move was backed by Opposition Leader Bill Shorten, who said in August 2014 at the Garma Festival in the Northern Territory: '[T]he sooner our Constitution honours the people who have shared an unbroken connection with this ancient continent – the better'. Shorten also said that constitutional recognition has to involve more than a token gesture: 'We need substantive and substantial change. Symbolic change is not good enough ...

Many Indigenous people have made it clear to me that they believe banning racism in our Constitution is vital'.[19]

In March 2014, the Coalition government engaged former Deputy Prime Minister and National Party leader John Anderson to conduct the review into public support for constitutional recognition mandated by the Recognition Act. The government said it wanted to 'work towards a parliamentary and community consensus on referendum proposals and report on steps that can be taken to progress towards a successful referendum'. Parliament also formed a joint select parliamentary committee chaired by Indigenous members of Parliament, Liberal Ken Wyatt from Western Australia and Northern Territory Labor Senator Nova Peris, to advance the work of the Expert Panel.[20] The committee produced reports that settled on variations to the Expert Panel's recommendations. The government also signalled its intent to announce a draft amendment to the Constitution for public consultation in late 2014.

However, other events intervened. In September 2013, most Indigenous policy and programs were moved to the Department of Prime Minister and Cabinet, and in May 2014, the Indigenous Advancement Strategy (IAS) was announced. This 'consolidated' all the items and activities that had been moved into the Prime Minister's Department and cut $534.4 million from Indigenous programs, grants and activities.[21] This occurred with limited notice to Indigenous communities whose programs and activities were overnight disestablished.

This process – and then the decisions of the IAS itself – led to a significant disempowerment of Aboriginal organisations. The notion of constitutional recognition became repugnant to those communities and organisations whose funding was cut or depleted under this new policy. The outrage accelerated a growing backlash in the community against the well-funded 'Recognise' organisation, which was prosecuting a form of constitutional recognition at odds with Aboriginal aspirations and local communities' experience. The affected communities and organisations instead saw the notion of constitutional recognition in a new light as an opportunity to address their voicelessness and powerlessness.

This backlash became so significant that Noel Pearson, Patrick Dodson, Kirstie Parker (co-Chair of the National Congress of Australia's First Peoples) and Megan Davis visited Abbott to argue for another process that would enable comprehensive consultation with Aboriginal and Torres Strait Islander peoples. The Prime Minister resolved to meet with key leaders to discuss recognition. Thirty-nine leaders attended the meeting with the Prime Minister and Opposition Leader at Kirribilli in July 2015. The Aboriginal and Torres Strait Islander leaders selected to attend the summit met over the weekend prior to the meeting to agree on the direction of constitutional recognition. A Statement was drafted to convey to the Prime Minister and the Opposition Leader the parameters of reform that were acceptable.

The Kirribilli Statement issued by Aboriginal and Torres Strait Islander attendees after the meeting said:

[A]ny reform must involve substantive changes to the
Australian Constitution. It must lay the foundation
for the fair treatment of Aboriginal and Torres Strait
Islander peoples into the future.

A minimalist approach, that provides preambular recognition, removes section 25 and moderates the race power [section 51(xxvi)], does not go far enough and would not be acceptable to Aboriginal and Torres Strait Islander peoples.[22]

The leaders also recommended that there be an ongoing dialogue between Aboriginal and Torres Strait Islander peoples and the government to negotiate the proposal to be put to referendum, as well as engagement about the acceptability of the proposed question. To undertake this, the new Prime Minister, Malcolm Turnbull, established the Referendum Council, which was jointly appointed by the Prime Minister and Leader of the Opposition Bill Shorten on 7 December 2015. The Council then commenced its work, which would lead to the Uluru Statement from the Heart.

5

THE REFERENDUM COUNCIL AND ULURU PROCESS

The Referendum Council, created in late 2015, was asked to advise Prime Minister Malcolm Turnbull and Opposition Leader Bill Shorten on the next steps towards a referendum. Its remit was to consult with Australians nationally, including Indigenous-led consultations, and to advise of the options for a referendum proposal, the steps for finalising that proposal and a possible timetable.

The Council's work was distinguished by the 12 First Nations Regional Dialogues. These dialogues elicited a firm response to the question asked by the federal government: what is meaningful recognition to you? The dialogues were followed by a National Convention at Uluru that saw Indigenous representatives from across Australia come to hear and endorse the work of the dialogues. On 26 May 2017, the National Constitutional Convention revealed that all 12 Regional Dialogues had answered the question in the clearest terms: Indigenous peoples seek a constitutionally protected Voice to the Parliament.

The Referendum Council

The Referendum Council comprised 15 Indigenous and non-Indigenous members. It included the former Chief Justice of the High Court of Australia Murray Gleeson, Natasha Stott Despoja, Amanda Vanstone, Stan Grant, Patricia Anderson, Noel Pearson, Megan Davis and Patrick Dodson (until he joined the Australian Senate) and others. The Council was asked to lead a 'process for national consultations and community engagement about constitutional recognition, including a concurrent series of Indigenous designed and led consultations' and to report to the Prime Minister and the Leader of the Opposition on 'options for a referendum proposal, steps for finalising a proposal, and possible timing for a referendum'.[1]

The Council first met on 14 December 2015 with Prime Minister Malcolm Turnbull and the Leader of the Opposition Bill Shorten in attendance. It met on 11 subsequent occasions from 2015 to the conclusion of its work in 2017 after the Uluru Statement.

The Referendum Council in its early deliberations decided that emphasis must be placed on consultation with Indigenous communities. It decided to conduct regional meetings with Aboriginal and Torres Strait Islander peoples to ascertain their support for constitutional recognition. This reflected the understanding that the constitutional recognition process involves two parties, the party doing the recognising and the party being recognised. It is important that those 'to be recognised' participate equally in the process and that there is consensus on the model of recognition.

The Referendum Council formed an Indigenous sub-committee constituted by Aboriginal and Torres Strait Islander members of the Referendum Council. This sub-committee made decisions on the structure of the consultations, the location, the methodology and the substantive options to discuss.

One of the first concerns of the sub-committee was that 'consultation' had become a dirty word in Indigenous communities. This antagonism to 'tick a box' consultation conducted by Commonwealth and state bureaucracies had been predicted by the Aboriginal and Torres Strait Islander leaders at Kirribilli. They instead sought a 'dialogue'. This meant that a new methodology had to be developed to encourage active participation and to enable participants to feel in control of the process.

Another concern of the sub-committee was the efficacy and authority of decision-making in the dialogues. ATSIC had a traditional Western liberal model of election and representation that was based upon individuals and not culture. This led to concern that decisions were being made in ways that did not reflect Aboriginal culture, including the fact that it is a collective culture based upon the authority of elders.

Similarly, the National Congress of Australia's First Peoples that succeeded ATSIC as a representative body was a model of representation that lacked cultural authority. While there were 'chambers' that included Indigenous peak bodies and organisations, there was no chamber for First Nations. The Congress was an incorporated body under the Corporations Act that struggled to gain influence outside of the machinery of government.

By contrast, the post-*Mabo* native title era had seen a resurgence in communities seeking models of representation that involved their cultural grouping. For this reason, the sub-committee decided that during the dialogues, decisions needed to be made by those who had cultural authority. The sub-committee structured each dialogue so as to require 60 per cent of invitations to the dialogue as traditional owners and elders, 20 per cent local Aboriginal organisations, and 20 per cent Aboriginal individuals such as Stolen Generations, youth or grandmothers.

The invitation formula was also important because like all such processes, not every single person could take part. The sub-committee was seeking a robust representation of First Nations and community sentiment. After all, watershed statements such as the Bark Petitions, Barunga, Eva Valley, Kalkaringi, the Social Justice Package and the Council for Aboriginal Reconciliation did not involve all First Nations peoples.

The final concern for the sub-committee was to decide the options for constitutional recognition that could be discussed within each dialogue. The Terms of Reference stated that the purpose of the Council's work was to build upon the extensive work of the Expert Panel and the 2015 Joint Select Committee on Constitutional Recognition of Aboriginal and Torres Strait Islander Peoples. This meant that five forms of recognition would be examined in the dialogues:

1   Drafting a statement acknowledging Aboriginal and Torres Strait Islander peoples as the First Australians, and inserting it either in the Constitution or outside the Constitution, either as a preamble in a new head of power or in a statutory Declaration of Recognition.

2 Amending or deleting the 'race power' section 51(xxvi), and replacing it with a new head of power (which might contain a statement of acknowledgment as a preamble to that power) to enable the continuation of necessary laws with respect to Indigenous issues.

3 Inserting into the Constitution a prohibition against racial discrimination.

4 Providing for an Indigenous Voice to be heard by Parliament, and the right to be consulted on legislation and policy that affect Aboriginal and Torres Strait Islander peoples.

5 Agreement-making, or treaty, by way of a binding agreement negotiated between two parties: the state and First Nations.

The Regional Dialogues

The First Nations Regional Dialogues were convened from December 2016 to May 2017 in 12 locations from Hobart through to Broome and Thursday Island in the Torres Strait (with an additional regional meeting in Canberra). Their purpose was to ensure that Aboriginal decision-making was at the heart of the process. This was in stark contrast to how many First Nations communities had been disenfranchised to date. This change of approach meant that, while the dialogue required information sessions such as civics knowledge, history and legal education on the recognition proposals, the participants drove decision-making on priorities for reform in each region.

To ensure a robust sample of community sentiment, each dialogue was conducted in the same way. This meant the agenda was the same for each. The dialogue was structured as a deliberative decision-making process that engaged participants in a discussion.

Each dialogue opened with an address by Patricia Anderson AO as the chair of the Referendum Council. The local leaders who led the dialogue then opened the proceedings with housekeeping and the agenda for the three days. Next, the group watched a short documentary, written by Megan Davis and produced and voiced by Rachel Perkins, which showed the lengthy history of advocacy for structural reform in Australia for Indigenous peoples. Following this, the group met together to discuss the key question: what is meaningful recognition to you in your region?

The next day focused on the law reform proposals. Megan Davis had written a civics script and Rachel Perkins had produced it to provide information about how the Australia legal and political system works. This included the difference between a Bill and an Act of Parliament and the difference between legislation and the Constitution. This session also included discussion on the accountability mechanisms built into the system to keep governments in check. It discussed the federal system and how the Constitution distributes power across the nation, ranging from shared powers to the exclusive power of the federal Parliament. The description of powers included the races power as amended in the historic 1967 referendum. The civics documentary also set out the role of the High Court as the ultimate interpreter of the meaning of the Constitution and how that document can be amended.

Break-out groups were then conducted, with each devoted to a single option. Then, a plenary session ventilated the reactions, ideas and criticism of each option. Following this, a second round of working groups was held, but this time the groups were cross-pollinated with people from each option. In the evening, people could discuss and debate options, and then sleep on them. The next morning, a draft Record of Meeting was prepared based on all the butcher's paper and whiteboard records before all participants signed off on the Record of Meeting.

This Record of Meeting was not shared with the following dialogues. One of the principles underpinning the method was to avoid groupthink. In group discussions, it is often the loudest voices in a room who are heard. This deters others from participating or expressing their views. It was important that for the purposes of free, prior and informed consent, people were able to participate freely without any particular ideology or agenda dominating. The Record of Meeting was the document that showed agreement, disagreement or tension on particular matters. It also showed the prioritisation of the reforms by the regional delegates and which reforms were viewed as an urgent priority and which were not.

At the conclusion of each Regional Dialogue, nominees were sought to attend the National Constitutional Convention at Uluru. In some of the dialogues, nominees were invited to address the group as to why they should attend the National Convention, and a vote was taken; in others, names were placed on a board or wall. Ten delegates were chosen to represent their region. This process of identifying delegates allowed the cultural authority that had been highlighted through the dialogue process to continue at the Uluru National Convention. The continuity of knowledge was also critical.

The National Constitutional Convention

The National Convention was held on 23–26 May 2017 at Yulara and Mutitjulu, near Uluru. Around 250 delegates attended from around Australia. At the opening ceremony, held at Mutitjulu, people from Arnhem Land and the Torres Strait, and Anangu men, the traditional owners of the land that the Convention was to meet on, performed three ceremonial dances. Over the next three days, delegates read out the Records of Meeting, conducted working groups on the key reforms and workshopped the way forward to a referendum.

The Convention endorsed the work of the dialogues. Although post-Uluru reporting suggests that there were votes on reforms and other such things, Uluru was only an endorsement meeting. The purpose of the national meeting was to hear the findings of each of the dialogues and to see where the results of the dialogues showed a clear consensus.

The Regional Dialogues ranked a Voice to Parliament as the first reform priority. The table opposite shows the preferences recorded in the Records of Meeting from each dialogue. Although not on the agenda put before the dialogues, truth-telling also emerged with unanimous support at every dialogue.

Reform priorities resulting from the Regional Dialogues

	Acknowledgment	Head of Power	Prohibition on Racial Discrimination	A Voice to Parliament	Agreement-making
Hobart	Not endorsed	Endorsed	Endorsed	Endorsed	Endorsed
Broome	Inconclusive	Endorsed	Not recorded	Endorsed	Not recorded
Dubbo	Not endorsed	Inconclusive	Not recorded	Endorsed	Endorsed
Darwin	Not endorsed	Endorsed	Endorsed	Endorsed	Endorsed
Perth	Not endorsed	Endorsed	Endorsed	Endorsed	Endorsed
Sydney	Inconclusive	Endorsed	Endorsed	Endorsed	Endorsed
Melbourne	Not endorsed	Not recorded	Not recorded	Endorsed	Endorsed
Cairns	Inconclusive	Endorsed	Not recorded	Endorsed	Endorsed
Ross River	Inconclusive	Inconclusive	Endorsed	Endorsed	Endorsed
Adelaide	Inconclusive	Endorsed	Not recorded	Endorsed	Endorsed
Brisbane	Inconclusive	Not endorsed	Endorsed	Endorsed	Endorsed
Thursday Island	Not endorsed	Inconclusive	Endorsed	Endorsed	Endorsed
Canberra	Not endorsed	Not recorded	Not recorded	Not recorded	Not recorded

Key:

Not endorsed	Endorsed	Inconclusive	Not recorded

Many of the proposals suggested by the Expert Panel did not feature prominently in the Regional Dialogue priorities, even though they were central to discussions.

The Regional Dialogues regarded section 25 of the Constitution, which recognises that states can prevent people from voting in their elections on the basis of race, as a dead letter. Its removal would be highly symbolic but without substantive benefit for Aboriginal and Torres Strait Islander peoples. The fact it was not prioritised is testament to the general approach of the dialogues, which was to not clutter a referendum with excessive amounts of symbolism. Participants were determined to settle on reform that would change lives.

This sentiment influenced decision-making on the races power. The multiple approaches to the races power were all ranked low or rejected in the dialogues. This was later lamented by federal Parliament's Joint Select Committee on Constitutional Recognition of Aboriginal and Torres Strait Islander Peoples. However, the conversation in the dialogues was that if no one could provide them with a rock-solid guarantee that an amended section 51(xxvi) or a section 51A could stop adverse discriminatory legislation, the change was the same as the status quo. Removing the word 'race' and inserting 'Aboriginal and Torres Strait Islander Peoples' would not change the possibility that Parliament would pass legislation that discriminated against Indigenous peoples. Participants at the dialogues were also alarmed that altering or deleting section 51(xxvi) could undermine beneficial legislation, particularly the *Native Title Act 1993*.

The Referendum Council extrapolated guiding principles from the dialogues to assist discussion of reforms at the National Convention at Uluru and to frame negotiations with the government following Uluru. The guiding principles enabled the reforms to be assessed according to fundamental values expressed by the dialogues.

In coming to these principles, the Council looked to historical statements of aspirations by Aboriginal and Torres Strait Islander peoples – including the Bark Petitions of 1963, the Barunga Statement of 1988, the Eva Valley Statement of 1993, the Kalkaringi Statement of 1998, the report on the Social Justice Package by ATSIC in 1995 and the Kirribilli Statement of 2015, as well as the United Nations Declaration on the Rights of Indigenous Peoples.

The principles were that a reform proposal could only succeed at Uluru if it:

- Does not diminish Aboriginal sovereignty and Torres Strait Islander sovereignty.
- Involves substantive, structural reform.
- Advances self-determination and the standards established under the United Nations Declaration on the Rights of Indigenous Peoples.
- Recognises the status and rights of First Nations.
- Tells the truth of history.
- Does not foreclose on future advancement.
- Does not waste the opportunity of reform.
- Provides a mechanism for First Nations agreement-making.
- Has the support of First Nations.
- Does not interfere with positive legal arrangements.[2]

A handful of delegates left the Convention because they preferred a treaty to constitutional reform. One of these people was Lidia Thorpe, who, in 2020, became a Senator for the Australian Greens and later an Independent. The more than 200 other delegates endorsed and respected the process of the Regional Dialogues, and drafted and adopted the Uluru Statement from the Heart.

The consensus that emerged at Uluru was for a sequenced reform process known as 'Voice, Treaty, Truth'. We examine these reforms in the next chapter. At the end of the Convention, on 26 May 2017, Megan Davis read out the Uluru Statement from the Heart for the first time, which is set out in full in appendix 1 to this book (see pages 192–93). It was addressed by the delegates to the Australian people, not Australian politicians. This was decided after much deliberation, the delegates believing that too many such processes resulted in Aboriginal and Torres Strait Islander peoples handing over a statement or petition or declaration to the Australian government, often in the form of a painting on bark or other material, that is then taken back to Canberra to hang on the walls of Parliament House rather than being acted upon.

Instead, it was decided to ask the Australian people to 'walk with us in a movement of the Australian people for a better future'. This was because the Constitution can be changed by Australians. It happened in 1967. And like 1967, Aboriginal and Torres Strait Islander peoples felt that Indigenous people and the wider Australian community could work together again to change the nation. The Uluru Statement provides the logic for the reform. Delegates felt convinced that if Australians read the Uluru Statement, they would understand the urgency of the task and would support change at the ballot box to benefit the entire nation.

Consultation with the broader community

In addition to the Regional Dialogues and the National Constitutional Convention, the Referendum Council solicited the views of all Australians. This happened through online consultation, telephone survey participation and written submissions.

Through the online mechanisms, 195 831 people actively engaged in the discussion.[3] In addition, 5300 people participated in online and telephone surveys conducted between November 2016 and May 2017. This included two samples of 2500 Australians representative of Australia's diverse geography and demography, as well as 100 Australians identifying as Aboriginal and/or Torres Strait Islander.

The Council also called for public submissions, based on a discussion paper. A total of 1111 submissions were received between December 2016 and May 2017.

A large majority of submissions supported all five of the key proposals. This included 93 per cent backing the inclusion of an Indigenous voice when Parliament and government make laws and policies about Indigenous affairs, 91 per cent supporting a statement of acknowledgment of Aboriginal and Torres Strait Islander peoples as the First Peoples of Australia, and 78 per cent in favour of a constitutional prohibition against racial discrimination.

Report of the Referendum Council

After the Uluru National Convention and the process of public consultation had concluded, the Referendum Council handed down its final report on 30 June 2017. The report reflected the strengths of the dialogue process and the clarity that this produced. It stated:

> The integrity of the process is evidenced in the fact that the exhaustive deliberations and informed participation of participants in the First Nations Regional Dialogues led to consensus at Uluru. The outcome captured in the Uluru Statement from the Heart was a testament to the efficacy of the structured process, which allowed the wisdom and intent of the representatives of the First Nations Regional Dialogues to coalesce in a common position.[4]

The First Nations Regional Dialogues placed Indigenous peoples at the forefront of the process. This was the opposite of how the Australian Constitution had been drafted. The Referendum Council explained it in this way:

> This process is unprecedented in our nation's history and is the first time a constitutional convention has been convened with and for First Peoples ... The Dialogues engaged 1200 Aboriginal and Torres Strait Islander delegates – an average of 100 delegates from each Dialogue – out of a population of approximately 600,000 people nationally. This is the most

proportionately significant consultation process
that has ever been undertaken with First Peoples.
Indeed, it engaged a greater proportion of the relevant
population than the constitutional convention
debates of the 1800s, from which First Peoples were
excluded.[5]

The Council endorsed the statement at Uluru and the call
for Voice, Treaty, Truth. It concluded:

> In consequence of the First Nations Regional
> Dialogues, the Council is of the view that the only
> option for a referendum proposal that accords with
> the wishes of Aboriginal and Torres Strait Islander
> Peoples is that which has been described as providing,
> in the Constitution, for a Voice to Parliament.[6]

The process undertaken by the Referendum Council was
very different from that undertaken by the Expert Panel,
and so a different result emerged. While the Expert Panel
chose the options for reform and then consulted, the reform
agenda produced at Uluru was the result of a ground-up,
deliberative decision-making process involving 12 Regional
Dialogues conducted around Australia. This provided clarity
and certainty about a singular option for reform that for the
first time had the backing of Indigenous peoples. The process
was also underpinned by cultural authority, particularly
from the traditional owners involved in the Regional Dialogue process. These factors underpinned the Referendum
Council recommendation that the Voice be put to the
people as a constitutional referendum.

The Referendum Council also recommended other non-constitutional changes that emerged from the Uluru Statement. These were an extra-constitutional statement of recognition, the establishment of a Makarrata commission to supervise agreement-making, and a process for truth-telling. The Council noted that these proposed reforms were modest and substantive, reasonable, unifying and capable of attracting the necessary support from both people and politicians.

Political responses

The Uluru Statement from the Heart immediately attracted national attention once it was issued to the Australian people on 26 May 2017. In the years since, it has been a focal point for debate about how the Constitution should be changed to realise Indigenous aspirations and to build a system of law and government that gives Aboriginal and Torres Strait Islander peoples a say over the issues that affect them.

Despite the strength of the dialogue process under-pinning the Statement and strong community support for its recommendations, the Statement encountered significant obstacles. On 26 October 2017, four months after the Uluru Convention, Prime Minister Turnbull rejected the idea of the Voice to Parliament. In a statement issued with the Attorney-General and the Minister for Indigenous Affairs, Nigel Scullion, the Prime Minister said: 'The Government does not believe such an addition to our national representative institutions is either desirable or capable of winning acceptance in a referendum'.[7]

He also argued that the Australian democracy is built on 'having equal civic rights' to 'vote for, stand for and serve in' either the House of Representatives or the Senate, and that 'a constitutionally enshrined additional representative assembly for which only Indigenous Australians could vote for or serve in is inconsistent with this fundamental principle'. He said that the Voice 'would inevitably become seen as a third chamber of Parliament'.

Although the Coalition government rejected the Voice to Parliament, there was agreement between the government and the opposition late in 2017 that there would be a Joint Select Committee of Parliament to consider the work of the Referendum Council. The two co-chairs, Labor Senator Patrick Dodson and Liberal Senator Julian Leeser, handed down a final report in November 2018. Their committee recommended that the government 'initiate a process of co-design [of the Voice] with Aboriginal and Torres Strait Islander peoples', followed by the government considering 'in a deliberate and timely manner, legislative, executive and constitutional options to establish The Voice'.[8]

As the 2019 federal election approached, the Labor Party made it party policy to support the Uluru Statement from the Heart and the Voice. They agreed with the Referendum Council that a referendum could be held based on the information from the dialogues, the council report and the decade-long process, and that the details of what the Voice looks like would be deferred to Parliament at a later date. They committed to put this to a referendum within the first term of a Labor government. Instead, the Coalition was returned to government at the May 2019 election after Scott Morrison became Prime Minister in 2018.

The incoming Minister for Indigenous Australians, Ken Wyatt, the first Indigenous person to hold the portfolio, announced in October 2019 a 'co-design' process for an 'Indigenous voice to government'. This would be a legislated body rather than a constitutionally entrenched one. Wyatt also announced that he wanted to put a referendum to the Australian public on constitutional recognition within the current term of Parliament.[9] He said that the Morrison Coalition government is 'committed to recognising Indigenous Australians in the constitution and working to achieve this through a process of true co-design'.[10]

It was not made clear what form this referendum would take, and whether this will be a minimalist and symbolic constitutional recognition and how it would work with a legislated Voice – that is, a Voice that is not placed within the Constitution as the Uluru Statement calls for. It might have been a process of legislating the Voice first and then constitutionally enshrining it later.

The 'co-design' process involved a Senior Advisory Group co-chaired by Marcia Langton and Tom Calma tasked with advising the Minister 'on the co-design process to develop options and models for an Indigenous voice to government'.[11] There was also a National Co-Design Group (which examined a national Voice, including the structure, operations, functions and membership of such a Voice) and a Local and Regional Co-Design Group (which developed options for 'local and regional voices'). These groups worked alongside a 'Senior Officials Group', consisting of representatives from state, territory and federal governments and the Australian Local Government Association.

The process culminated in a 272-page final report delivered to Wyatt in July 2021. It described 'a cohesive and integrated system comprised of Local & Regional Voices and a National Voice – with connections to existing Aboriginal and Torres Strait Islander bodies'.[12] It did not recommend whether this new model should be legislated or placed in the Constitution via a referendum, as such questions were excluded from its terms of reference. The report did, however, note that:

> We heard many practical and principled reasons supporting the enshrinement of an Indigenous Voice in the Australian Constitution, including that it would be the best way to protect an Indigenous Voice against abolition, enhance its effectiveness and recognise the unique place of Aboriginal and Torres Strait Islander peoples in our nation. Security and longevity for an Indigenous Voice were crucial elements of feedback received across the consultation process. The task for government is to consider how the Indigenous Voice will be protected.[13]

The co-design report proposed 25 to 35 Local and Regional Voices across Australia to undertake community engagement, provide advice to, and work in partnership with all levels of government. They would work together to set strategic directions to improve policy, program and service delivery outcomes for communities in the regions and provide joint advice about how investment can be better aligned to local priorities and strategies.

A flexible approach would allow 'the breadth of functions, membership and governance arrangements to be decided locally'.[14]

The report suggested the National Voice be a small body comprising 24 Aboriginal and Torres Strait Islander members to advise the Australian Parliament and Government so that 'Aboriginal and Torres Strait Islander peoples have a direct say on any national laws, policies and programs affecting them'.[15] Local and Regional Voices would determine National Voice members from their area to 'embed community voices and ensure the diversity of Aboriginal and Torres Strait Islander communities is connected to the National Voice'.[16]

The Morrison government did not act upon its co-design report by legislating for a Voice to Government or holding a referendum prior to the May 2022 federal election. Instead, Prime Minister Morrison ruled out a referendum enshrining a Voice in the Constitution if his party was re-elected. By contrast, the Labor Party led by Opposition Leader Anthony Albanese again committed itself to implementing the Uluru Statement from the Heart, including by holding a referendum in its first term of office to bring about a Voice to Parliament.

6

VOICE, TREATY, TRUTH

The Uluru Statement from the Heart called for a constitutionally protected Voice to Parliament, Treaty and Truth. The reforms are listed in a sequence. The sequence is deliberate, and understanding the order is central to the message of the Uluru Statement. It was based upon recognition that public institutions, politicians and political parties rarely listen to what Indigenous peoples say about their lives and aspirations. Too often these bodies rewrite, reinterpret and rearrange the things that First Peoples themselves say on matters of reform.

The sequence:
Voice, then Treaty and Truth

The process was predicated on an amendment to the text of the Australian Constitution through a referendum of the Australian people. The Voice to Parliament is that reform. A treaty does not require constitutional amendment, nor does 'truth-telling', at least in the way treaty and truth were contemplated by those involved in the dialogues.

The Voice to Parliament is a structural reform. It is a change to the structure of Australia's public institutions and would redistribute public power via the Constitution, Australia's highest law. The reform will create an institutional relationship between governments and First Nations that will compel the state to listen to Aboriginal and Torres Strait Islander peoples in policy- and decision-making.

The next phase of the sequence of the Uluru reforms is a Makarrata, a process of agreement-making and truth-telling. Treaty has been a long-time aspiration for Aboriginal people. Negotiating a treaty is a nation-to-nation process that requires leverage and resources. Having a Voice to Parliament will increase the likelihood that treaty negotiations will be productive and successful.

The Voice will be an enabling mechanism for First Nations people in any treaty negotiations. Aboriginal and Torres Strait Islander peoples are in a poor negotiating position compared to the state. The Voice would create the Commission that will support First Nations in those negotiations. Without the Voice, a treaty is vulnerable because of the considerable legal power of the Commonwealth. State treaty processes are also particularly vulnerable, including those that are ongoing in Australia. Each runs the risk of being undermined by the Commonwealth.

Voice to Parliament

The First Nations Regional Dialogues unanimously ranked a Voice to the Australian Parliament as the number one priority in their region and for constitutional recognition.

The idea of a Voice to Parliament stems from the experience of many Indigenous peoples globally who seek to find pragmatic and functional ways of influencing government. After all, many Indigenous peoples are vulnerable to the state, whose laws and policies often shape the way their lives are lived.

Democracies also function in a way that centres elections as the primary method by which community sentiment is determined. And the ballot box, based upon free and fair periodic elections, is a numbers game, given that the representative with the greatest number of votes wins the opportunity to represent the community. The numbers game of elections plays against Indigenous peoples' issues. Aboriginal and Torres Strait Islander peoples may be the 'First Peoples', but they are less than 3 per cent of the Australian population. Majority vote at the ballot box and in Parliament means it is difficult for their voice to be heard and for them to influence laws that are made about them. It is not surprising, then, that Indigenous peoples have argued for political representation and fairer consultation for more than a century.

In 2007, the United Nations General Assembly adopted a framework of Indigenous peoples' rights that reflected global agreement on the minimum standards that should be afforded by the state. In 2009, Australia endorsed the United Nations Declaration on the Rights of Indigenous Peoples, which emphasises the importance of genuine Indigenous participation and consultation in political decisions made about their rights. However, no formal processes for this to occur have yet been implemented in Australia.

The United Nations Declaration on the Rights of

Indigenous Peoples sets out treaties and agreements as separate to the kind of constitutional power envisaged by the Voice. Treaties, agreements and other constructive arrangements are critical for the state and Indigenous peoples to negotiate partnership and rights. These may be recognised constitutionally, legislatively or by way of private law in contract. However, they are separate and in addition to the kind of structural power enabled by constitutional recognition for the Voice.

While a treaty might contemplate issues that are exclusively for First Nations to lead on, the reality is that most matters will have some input from different levels of government. The idea behind a Voice to Parliament is that Aboriginal and Torres Strait Islander peoples are engaged in the development and implementation of laws, policies and programs that always affect them and their rights. This is the only way to achieve better quality policies and laws and a fairer relationship with government. This is one of the compelling reasons the First Nations dialogues thought the Constitution should be amended by establishing an Indigenous body – as many other countries have – to advise Parliament on laws and policies relating to Indigenous affairs. Such a body would ensure that the views of First Peoples are heard by lawmakers and could help Parliament enact better and more effective laws.

Other countries with a similar structure include Norway, Sweden and Finland, which all have a First Nations Parliament with various degrees of authority over some matters and a right to be consulted on legislation. In New Zealand, there are seven seats reserved in Parliament for Māori people. In Colombia, there is a constitutional provision that requires government to consult with Indigenous peoples before allowing natural resource exploitation on Indigenous lands. These examples, and the proposed Voice in Australia, are all consistent with the United Nations Declaration on the Rights of Indigenous Peoples, particularly Article 18, which states that: 'Indigenous peoples have the right to participate in decision-making in matters which would affect their rights, through representatives chosen by themselves in accordance with their own procedures, as well as to maintain and develop their own indigenous decision-making institutions'.

The First Nations dialogues also discussed how a structural change of this form could prevent Parliament passing discriminatory laws and policies. If the race power in section 51(xxvi) of the Constitution were to be replaced or amended, Aboriginal people and Torres Strait Islanders would need some assurance that any new or amended power could only be used positively or for their advancement or benefit. The use of the Voice to address the concerns of Indigenous peoples about possible discriminatory legislation being passed by the federal Parliament was a solution devised in the dialogues.

This is how the Voice emerged as a preferred option to section 116A, the non-discrimination clause recommended by the Expert Panel. Section 116A was ranked high in the prioritisation of options by the First Nations regional dialogues. However, section 116A was more passive than the Voice because it could only be used if and when the government passed racially discriminatory laws. This meant that section 116A would not empower people to be actively involved upfront in the political process. Section 116A was more of a shield than a sword. If the federal Parliament passed a discriminatory law, litigation would be required to test the law, which would involve considerable financial outlay for communities and emotional costs associated with the lengthy wait and uncertainty. The Voice was considered a more effective institution to empower Indigenous communities and provide a check on Parliament.

The idea that a Voice could scrutinise or monitor the Commonwealth's use of power as it relates to Indigenous peoples is not new in Australia's constitutional system. There are many mechanisms that inform and advise the federal Parliament on such matters. The Productivity Commission, the Australian Law Reform Commission, the Auditor-General and the Australian National Audit Office are examples. Another example of such monitoring work is the scrutiny of proposed laws under the *Human Rights (Parliamentary Scrutiny) Act 2011*. All of these mechanisms are intended to improve the quality of law- and policy-making by the Commonwealth. As constitutional law professor Anne Twomey has said:

> It is hard to imagine that anyone would argue that it is better for Parliament to be ignorant and ill-informed, its laws ineffective and its expenditure wasteful. There can be no harm in listening to the views of others and using them to improve outcomes.[1]

The proposal for a Voice emerged with great enthusiasm and wide support in response to the vacuum of political representation for Indigenous peoples that had emerged after the abolition of ATSIC. In the 2014 Nugget

Coombs oration, Marion Scrymgour, a former ATSIC Commissioner, spoke about a special advisory body made up of Indigenous representatives that would have input into government decisions affecting Aboriginal people. The idea of a constitutional advisory function or a duty to consult was also foreshadowed in the Kirribilli Statement as a possible option for a constitutional advisory body.

In 2015, a federal parliamentary committee added a constitutional advisory function to its list of alternative forms of constitutional recognition outside of the Expert Panel recommendations. That committee had the benefit of substantive submissions from the Cape York Institute, which had spent half a decade developing the proposal, including studying the Waitangi Tribunal and Māori legal and political recognition, as well as the Sami Parliaments in Finland, Norway and Sweden. This reflected the view of Aboriginal lawyer Noel Pearson that effective recognition meant giving Indigenous peoples a better say in the democratic processes affecting their affairs.

Such reforms have been frequently suggested over the years. The Barunga Statement in 1988 called for '[a] national elected Aboriginal and Islander organisation to oversee Aboriginal and Islander affairs'. The Barunga Statement also called for 'the Commonwealth Parliament to negotiate with us a Treaty recognising our prior ownership, continued occupation and sovereignty and affirming our human rights and freedom'.

The calls for reform over the past century reveal advocacy for a voice within the democratic framework of the state as a pragmatic way of First Nations adapting to the legal and political environment imposed upon them. There is also advocacy for a framework for a treaty that would enable communities to practise self-determination. This two-tier approach is common in countries with significant Indigenous populations to ensure every possible mechanism can be adopted to influence the state and to leverage public power to drive change in communities.

The idea of enshrinement or constitutional protection of the Voice is key to the capacity of communities to drive change. Each First Nations dialogue spoke to the need for this Voice to be durable and sustainable and so to exist beyond any one political cycle. Many lamented the fact that Indigenous affairs was a 'political football' and that Indigenous issues are subject to political whim. Communities saw the ideological nature of Indigenous affairs as being one reason why there is so much entrenched disadvantage.

Some First Nations dialogue participants spoke about the business, pastoralist and farmer demands for 'certainty' after the *Mabo* decision by the High Court of Australia, and said this applies equally to Indigenous affairs. They felt that they should equally have some certainty from one political cycle to the next about their funding and programs. This would enable communities to plan for the future and strategise for a longer term beyond the three-year period between federal elections.

The Referendum Council report made its recommendation for the Voice in the following terms:

That a referendum be held to provide in the Australian Constitution for a representative body that gives Aboriginal and Torres Strait Islander First Nations a Voice to the Commonwealth Parliament. One of the specific functions of such a body, to be set out in legislation outside the Constitution, should include the function of monitoring the use of the heads of power in section 51(xxvi) and section 122 [the territories power]. The body will recognise the status of Aboriginal and Torres Strait Islander Peoples as the First Peoples of Australia.[2]

The Referendum Council recommended that the Constitution be amended to create a Voice to Parliament. It did not recommend enshrining an entire model. Instead, the detail would be deferred to Parliament. Getting the balance right is challenging. Too little detail may not be sufficient for an informed vote, while too much detail may be problematic in not leaving flexibility for Parliament to decide how the Voice will work and to adapt this over time.

One approach identified by the Referendum Council is to hold the referendum first and design the Voice later. Another approach is to design it first so people have a model in mind that Parliament might enact after the referendum. This could help Australians make a more informed decision at the ballot box and allay concerns about what the Voice might look like.

The idea of leaving the design of an institution later to Parliament was used by the Australian drafters of the Constitution when they created the High Court of Australia. They enshrined the Court in the Constitution, and it was designed and passed in legislation a few years later. Referendums are the same. The rules in section 128 set up the referendum and defers detail on the referendum to Parliament. This is consistent with what former High Court Chief Justice Murray Gleeson has said about the design of the Voice:

> The structure, composition and functions of [the Voice] would be determined, and susceptible to change, by legislation of the Federal Parliament. What would appear in the Constitution would be the minimum requirements necessary to guarantee its continued existence and its essential characteristics.[3]

Within this framework, some aspects of the design of the Voice were still put forward. The Referendum Council Final Report said that the Voice must:

> have authority from, be representative of, and have legitimacy in Aboriginal and Torres Strait Islander communities across Australia. It must represent communities in remote, rural and urban areas, and not be comprised of handpicked leaders. The body must be structured in a way that respects culture. Any body must also be supported by a sufficient and guaranteed budget, with access to its own independent secretariat, experts and lawyers. It was also suggested that the body could represent Aboriginal and Torres Strait Islander Peoples internationally. A number of Dialogues said the body's representation could be drawn from an Assembly of First Nations, which could be established through a series of treaties among nations.[4]

The Voice as envisaged by many dialogues would be First Nations based, not individual based. First Nations based means that the electorates would be drawn from the collectives of Aboriginal nations countrywide. The collective is the way Aboriginal culture exists. The people eligible would likely be the body of traditional owners, which means that members of the Voice represent their cultural authority. This would render the decision-making of the Voice very serious and deeply embedded in communities. One thing each dialogue had said was that the sector peak bodies who do service delivery in communities are not representative of communities and are not their voice. There was some tension about how these bodies purport to represent community sentiment to politicians in Canberra but never report back. This means there is very little accountability.

The dialogues proposed that the First Nations themselves would determine how they are represented. This would occur in line with their right to self-determination via a further national dialogue process that allowed them to drive design (rather than merely consultation on a pre-designed model).

On the question of representation, all groups said the model must be First Nations based, but some groups in dialogues expressed a commitment to liberal democratic governance and said that the selection of a cultural authority among a group should be conducted by ballot box elections. This would mean engaging, as did ATSIC and the National Congress of Australia's First Peoples, the Australian Electoral Commission to supervise elections. Other First Nations could immediately identify who had the cultural authority to represent them. Others might seek to retain existing mechanisms of statutory land rights or native title such as prescribed body corporates. Concerns about manageable numbers saw other First Nations contemplate cultural authority via regional groupings.

Where conversations turned to how many people might make up the Voice, some said 200 representatives in an Assembly and some said 72. Either way, it was agreed that institutional design should not be led by the question: what is the right number for the Voice to be manageable? They felt that this question serves bureaucrats and governments who seek a manageable number for their own processes. They pointed to governments relying upon a few unrepresentative leaders in the absence of ATSIC's 32 representatives and 12-member national board.

It was clear during the dialogues that Indigenous grass-roots communities felt disempowered and voiceless and did not believe that the many structures and groups that surround them are representing their thoughts and needs and wants. This also reflected poor outcomes from political leaders and bureaucracies. There was a very clear aspiration to have a direct connection between Canberra and community. There was little appetite for generalist elections, whereby those with sophisticated Western-style résumés are more appealing than those without. ATSIC was spoken of as having had a regional governance model that worked well because it was drawn from people who lived in communities and regions, not capital cities. It was felt that the Voice could follow this path to accommodate the diverse ways in which First Nations express their cultural authority and legitimacy.

It was felt that to achieve this the Voice must be entrenched in the Constitution. Doing so would ensure that the Voice is not subject to easy repeal by Parliament. The Referendum Council noted that a constitutionally entrenched Voice was important to participants in the Regional Dialogues and the National Convention:

> because of the history of poor or nonexistent consultation with communities by the Commonwealth. Consultation is either very superficial or it is more meaningful, but then wholly ignored.
>
> For Dialogue participants, the logic of a constitutionally enshrined Voice – rather than a legislative body alone – is that it provides reassurance and recognition that this new norm of participation and consultation would be different to the practices of the past.[5]

Treaty

The second reform called for in the First Nations Regional Dialogues was a Makarrata commission to oversee a process of agreement-making and truth-telling. As we saw in chapter 3, the Yolngu word Makarrata ('the coming together after a struggle' or 'things are all right again after a conflict') was adopted by the treaty campaign in the 1970s. The term 'agreement-making' is interchangeable with 'treaty'. It means a binding agreement between a First Nation and the state that has legal effect and is aimed at resolving difficult problems by negotiation rather than fighting things out in court or governments imposing top-down legislation.

Treaty, or agreement-making, has been an ambition of many Aboriginal and Torres Strait Islander people for decades. However, federal governments have mostly ignored this call. There was some interest in a treaty under the government of Prime Minister Malcolm Fraser, and Bob Hawke committed to a treaty as Prime Minister. This became a broken promise. At the time of the Referendum Council's work, Victoria and South Australia were actively pursuing treaty agreements. However, such processes depend upon the government of the day and its political priorities. South Australia had a treaty process under a Labor government that began in 2016, but when that government lost office in 2018, the treaty process was abandoned. The South Australian treaty talks were restarted when Labor returned to office in 2022. Queensland, Tasmania, New South Wales, the Northern Territory and the Australian Capital Territory have also committed to treaty talks with their Indigenous communities. Only Western Australia has yet to begin a comprehensive treaty process.

Pursuing a treaty or treaties was strongly supported in the dialogues and at the National Convention because this course of action has always been viewed as an important path to reconciliation. The dialogues in the official record of discussion described it in this way:

> [T]here is Unfinished Business to resolve. And the
> way to address these differences is through agreement-
> making.

'Treaty was seen as the best form of establishing an honest relationship with government.'
(Dubbo)

Makarrata is another word for Treaty or agreement-making. It is the culmination of our agenda. It captures our aspirations for a fair and honest relationship with government and a better future for our children based on justice and self-determination.

'If the community can't self-determine and make decisions for our own community regarding economic and social development, then we can't be confident about the future for our children.'
(Wreck Bay)

Through negotiated settlement, First Nations can build their cultural strength, reclaim control and make practical changes over the things that matter in their daily life. By making agreements at the highest level, the negotiation process with the Australian government allows First Nations to express our sovereignty – the sovereignty that we know comes from The Law.[6]

It was recognised at the Regional Dialogues that for a treaty process to occur, the community needs considerably more resources to engage with the state, as well as a lengthy period for planning. A number of dialogues referred to the Waitangi Tribunal in New Zealand/Aotearoa as an example of how an institutional body could assist communities in preparing to negotiate agreements.

The dialogues also discussed how state- and territory-based treaties are vulnerable to being overridden by the Commonwealth. The federal Parliament can override state and territory agreements using its races power and territories power. These treaties might also be overridden by future state parliaments because each treaty will most likely be an ordinary Act of Parliament. Dialogues discussed how lopsided a treaty would be in the absence of the Commonwealth. The Victorian treaty process, for example, has had to leave an entire section of the framework to one side because it involves the large number of matters that fall under the exclusive jurisdiction of the Commonwealth.

Many dialogues expressed hurt at the native title process and how it has torn communities apart and inflamed intracultural disputes and tensions. For this reason, many dialogues said that there needed to be a treaty 'with ourselves' or among each other in order to learn how to work together again.

Those who had participated in the native title system spoke about how disenfranchised they felt with that system. They said that the courts, native title services bodies and land councils that are ostensibly set up to protect and service Indigenous communities often fail to do so. Native title groups are under-resourced and are required to enter into agreements, such as Indigenous Land Use Agreements, where there is often a serious power imbalance. The sector attracts lawyers and other parties who can take advantage of impecunious communities at sea in a complex regulatory system.

Dialogue participants also expressed concern that the native title system, if not the entire ecosystem of Indigenous affairs, forces communities to 'incorporate' their affairs by creating a company structure. Much was said about the incongruous nature of Western-style incorporation and that communities become bogged down in procedural matters, such as minutes and board elections, and less time is spent on strategic and unifying activities that bring communities together. Both the *Corporations (Aboriginal and Torres Strait Islander) Act 2006* and the *Corporations Act 2001*, and accompanying regulators, were singled out for criticism in virtually all dialogues.

It is important to note that not all dialogues ranked Treaty highly. In the Broome dialogue, for example, many people expressed fatigue with agreement-making because so much of this was conducted once strong native title claims have been successful and recognised. There are also groups of activists known as sovereignty mobs and resistance mobs who do not want constitutional voice nor a treaty. They view all change as subjugating Aboriginal 'sovereignty' to the Crown. The importance of the dialogues process is that it elicited a complex and nuanced picture of communities across Australia. No one community is like another and no one person or group can speak for all communities. This showed the power of the dialogues in avoiding groupthink or pre-existing political agendas.

Truth

The final aspect of the sequence was truth-telling. During the dialogues, each region sought to speak first about their history and its place in the nation's story before they wanted to speak about the Constitution. Many made the point that you cannot recognise that which you do not know. Although truth-telling was not an option for reform that was put to the dialogues, it was clear to the Referendum Council that there was a desire in each community for there to be more emphasis on truth-telling.

The need for people to know more about Australian and Aboriginal history was repeatedly raised in the dialogues. Across Australia, the idea of history and truth-telling emerged as a strong theme. This led the Referendum Council to capture the richness in 'Our Story', the Aboriginal history of Australia that follows the one-page Uluru Statement from the Heart. This story commences:

> Our First Nations are extraordinarily diverse cultures, living in an astounding array of environments, multi-lingual across many hundreds of languages and dialects. The continent was occupied by our people and the footprints of our ancestors traversed the entire landscape. Our songlines covered vast distances, uniting peoples in shared stories and religion. The entire land and seascape is named, and the cultural memory of our old people is written there. This rich diversity of our origins was eventually ruptured by colonisation. Violent dispossession and the struggle to survive a relentless inhumanity has marked our common history. The First Nations Regional Dialogues on constitutional reform bore witness to our shared stories.

The truth-telling ventilated by 13 Regional Dialogues involved many facets of Australian history from Captain Cook to the brute force of the Protection Era and on to land rights and activism. On Captain Cook and the Australia story of nation, 'Our Story' says:

Australia was not a settlement and it was not a discovery.

It was an invasion.

'Cook did not discover us, because we saw him. We were telling each other with smoke, yet in his diary, he said "discovered".' (Torres Strait Regional Dialogue)

'Australia must acknowledge its history, its true history. Not Captain Cook. What happened all across Australia: the massacres and the wars. If that were taught in schools, we might have one nation, where we are all together.' (Darwin Regional Dialogue)

The invasion that started at Botany Bay is the origin of the fundamental grievance between the old and new Australians: that Australia was colonised without the consent of its rightful owners.

Now is an opportunity for the First Nations to tell the truth about history in our own voices and from our own point of view.

And for mainstream Australians to hear those voices
and to reconsider what they know and understand
about their nation's history. This will be challenging,
but the truth about invasion needs to be told.

Many dialogues then discussed how truth-telling had
been conducted in Australian legal and political contexts.
Over the last 30 years, several important truth-telling
processes have been carried out in Australia, particularly in
commissions and reports, including the Royal Commission
into Aboriginal Deaths in Custody, the *Bringing Them
Home* report on the Stolen Generations, the Australian
Law Reform Commission report into recognition of
Aboriginal customary law and the Council for Aboriginal
Reconciliation's final report. These show the many ways
the state has asked Indigenous peoples to tell their stories
to understand the truth of history to avoid repeating the
wrongs of the past. Despite this, Australia's understanding
of colonial history, the dispossession and the genocide, the
Frontier Wars and massacres, and discriminatory policies
are not well understood. One quote from the Ross River
dialogue demonstrates the importance of truth-telling:

> Participants expressed disgust about a statue of John
> McDouall Stuart being erected in Alice Springs
> following the 150th anniversary of his successful
> attempt to reach the Top End. This expedition led
> to the opening up of the 'South Australian frontier'
> which led to massacres as the telegraph line was
> established and white settlers moved into the region.
> People feel sad whenever they see the statue; its

presence and the fact that Stuart is holding a gun is disrespectful to the Aboriginal community who are descendants of the families slaughtered during the massacres throughout central Australia.[7]

Overall, the dialogues were overwhelmingly of the view that a nation cannot recognise people they do not know or understand.

Having said that, there was also a pragmatic view about the way power works in Canberra. Many were exhausted by the endless calls for Aboriginal people to give voice to truth-telling and their version of history. They also felt that this never alters or penetrates the national narrative and so viewed truth-telling as a way of delaying or avoiding the recognition of substantive and concrete rights. Many alluded to Prime Minister Bob Hawke's failed promise for a treaty and national land rights. When he did not deliver on treaty, he instead set up a statutory process for reconciliation so that Australians could get to know Aboriginal and Torres Strait Islander peoples better.

In light of this history, the dialogues did not demand a truth-telling process or a truth commission. They also did not want the opportunity of constitutional power through the Voice communities to be given up in favour of another truth-telling process that could drain people of their emotional energy and for which there would be no end in sight. They also discussed that there is no treaty process in the world that required a truth-telling process first.

There was a strong view that truth-telling is being done now but it needs more coordination. Statutory land rights and native title require First Nations people to collate their histories and stories. Many First Nations people do this on a daily basis with high schools, community groups, businesses and local historical societies. Many communities are also actively involved with local councils, which appear to be the heavy lifters in the federation on truth and reconciliation. From ceremonies for massacre sites, protection for sacred areas and memorials for significant events, much is committed at the local level. What was important to the communities was that truth-telling is done at their pace, when they are ready and that it is bottom-up. The notion of being compelled to tell your stories without any sense that the telling will be recognised in good faith was of concern. The many recommendations of important commissions and inquiries that have never been implemented are evidence of this.

The most common method of truth-telling backed by the First Nations dialogues was through the education system. There was a concern that primary school and high school teaching of Aboriginal history was not sufficient or thorough enough, and that school curricula needed to be changed. Other approaches, such as memorialising and public art, museums, cultural or educational healing centres and institutions, were also suggested. This truth-telling might be localised and could grow out of an agreement-making process and commence at any time.

7

THE VOICE

Labor made clear immediately on winning the May 2022 federal election that the nation was headed to a referendum on the Voice. On election night, incoming Prime Minister Anthony Albanese said that 'I commit to the Uluru Statement from the Heart in full'. He went on to say:

> [T]ogether we can embrace the Uluru Statement from the Heart.
>
> We can answer its patient, gracious call for a voice enshrined in our constitution. Because all of us ought to be proud that amongst our great multicultural society we count the oldest living continuous culture in the world.[1]

The Prime Minister followed up his words with a significant speech on 30 July 2022 at the Garma Festival in the Northern Territory. He called for a community discussion about recognition in the Constitution through a referendum on the Voice and set out draft wording for the reform:

Our starting point is a recommendation to add three sentences to the Constitution, in recognition of Aboriginal and Torres Strait Islanders as the First Peoples of Australia:

> 1. There shall be a body, to be called the Aboriginal and Torres Strait Islander Voice.

> 2. The Aboriginal and Torres Strait Islander Voice may make representations to Parliament and the Executive Government on matters relating to Aboriginal and Torres Strait Islander Peoples.

> 3. The Parliament shall, subject to this Constitution, have power to make laws with respect to the composition, functions, powers and procedures of the Aboriginal and Torres Strait Islander Voice.[2]

The Prime Minister's wording became the starting point for discussions over the following year on what the Voice would look like, and what form it should take in the Constitution.

Referendum working groups

Following the Garma speech, the government developed a process to lead the conversation about the legal change, the mechanics of the referendum and engagement with Indigenous communities and the Australian people. This was bolstered on 17 August 2022, when a meeting of Indigenous Affairs ministers from all states and territories and the Commonwealth agreed to support the process for the referendum on the Voice.

The government decided that the path to the referendum would be supported by three groups. A Referendum Working Group of Aboriginal and Torres Strait Islander peoples was the primary body to work with government and provide advice on the referendum proposal and how to ensure its success. It was supported by a Referendum Engagement Group of Indigenous peoples, which provided advice and opportunities for engagement to build community understanding, awareness and advocacy for the Voice, and a Constitutional Expert Group, comprising constitutional scholars and practitioners who advised on legal issues arising from drafting the change to the Constitution.

The first group to be constituted was the Referendum Working Group, co-chaired by Linda Burney, Minister for Indigenous Australians, and Senator Patrick Dodson, Special Envoy for Reconciliation and the Implementation of the Uluru Statement from the Heart. Importantly, the Albanese government elevated the voices of Indigenous peoples in establishing the Referendum Working Group. Its terms of reference stated that 'the Government considers it essential that Aboriginal and Torres Strait Islander voices are heard in the process leading up to and during the referendum'.[3]

The Referendum Working Group was informed by the work already undertaken over more than a decade of the journey to constitutional recognition. This included the the Expert Panel on Constitutional Recognition of Indigenous Australians (2012), the Joint Select Committee on Constitutional Recognition of Aboriginal and Torres Strait Islander Peoples (2015), the Referendum Council and Uluru Statement from the Heart (2017), the Joint Select Committee on Constitutional Recognition Relating to Aboriginal and Torres Strait Islander Peoples (2018) and the Indigenous Voice Co-design Process (2019–2021).

The Group began by determining what kind of detail is needed on the model prior to a referendum, taking into account that it will be the job of Parliament after the referendum to legislate about the operation of the Voice. Over six months, the Group developed principles to help frame the discussion about a Voice. In explaining what a Voice to Parliament is, the Group stated that it will be a permanent body to make representations to the Australian Parliament and the executive government on legislation and policy of significance to Aboriginal and Torres Strait Islander peoples. It also said the Voice will further the self-determination of Aboriginal and Torres Strait Islander peoples by giving them a greater say on matters that affect them. This was expressed in the following design principles agreed to by the Referendum Working Group and released to the public:

The Voice will give independent advice to the Parliament and government

- The Voice would make representations to the Parliament and the Executive Government on matters relating to Aboriginal and Torres Strait Islander peoples.

- The Voice would be able to make representations proactively.
- The Voice would be able to respond to requests for representations from the Parliament and the Executive Government.
- The Voice would have its own resources to allow it to research, develop and make representations.
- The Parliament and Executive Government should seek representations in writing from the Voice early in the development of proposed laws and policies.

The Voice will be chosen by Aboriginal and Torres Strait Islander people based on the wishes of local communities

- Members of the Voice would be selected by Aboriginal and Torres Strait Islander communities, not appointed by the Executive Government.
- Members would serve on the Voice for a fixed period of time, to ensure regular accountability to their communities.
- To ensure cultural legitimacy, the way that members of the Voice are chosen would suit the wishes of local communities and would be determined through the post-referendum process.

The Voice will be representative of Aboriginal and Torres Strait Islander communities, gender balanced and include youth

- Members of the Voice would be Aboriginal and/or Torres Strait Islander, according to the standard three-part test.
- Members would be chosen from each of the states, territories and the Torres Strait Islands.
- The Voice would have specific remote representatives as well as representation for the mainland Torres Strait Islander population.
- The Voice will have balanced gender representation at the national level.

The Voice will be empowering, community-led, inclusive, respectful and culturally informed

- Members of the Voice would be expected to connect with – and reflect the wishes of – their communities.
- The Voice would consult with grassroots communities and regional entities to ensure its representations are informed by their experience, including the experience of those who have been historically excluded from participation.

The Voice will be accountable and transparent

- The Voice would be subject to standard governance and reporting requirements to ensure transparency and accountability.
- Voice members would fall within the scope of the National Anti-Corruption Commission.
- Voice members would be able to be sanctioned or removed for serious misconduct.

The Voice will work alongside existing organisations and traditional structures

- The Voice would respect the work of existing organisations.

The Voice will not have a program delivery function

- The Voice would be able to make representations about improving programs and services, but it would not manage money or deliver services.

The Voice will not have a veto power [4]

At the final meeting of the Referendum Working Group in March 2023, it advised the government that the draft constitutional amendment announced by the Prime Minister at Garma in July 2022 was a 'solid foundation' for the Voice. It also recommended that:

- The following words be included at the beginning of the amendment: 'In recognition of Aboriginal and Torres Strait Islander peoples as the First Peoples of Australia'.
- The body be called the 'Aboriginal and Torres Strait Islander Voice'.
- The reference to 'Executive Government' be retained, and the provision should refer to the Parliament and the Executive Government 'of the Commonwealth'.
- The wording should be changed to make clear the broad scope of Parliament's power to make laws relating to the Voice.
- The amendment should be in a new section 129 of the Constitution titled 'Aboriginal and Torres Strait Islander Voice', which should be in a new Chapter IX of the Constitution titled 'Recognition of Aboriginal and Torres Strait Islander Peoples'.

The Referendum Working Group stated that:

> With these changes, the Working Group considers the Voice enshrined in the Constitution will be an unflinching source of advice and accountability to the Parliament and Executive Government. Such a constitutional amendment will also deliver on the aspirations of First Nations peoples for constitutional recognition through a Voice as set out in the Uluru Statement from the Heart.

The Group also said that the question put to voters on the ballot paper should 'be as simple and as clear as possible' and should include a reference to the recognition of the 'First Peoples of Australia'.[5] This would enable the question to speak to the substantive and symbolic aspects of change.

The change to the Constitution

On 23 March 2023, Prime Minister Albanese announced the government's preferred wording for the constitutional amendment to be put to the Australian people, as agreed to by the Referendum Working Group. This was contained in a Bill introduced into Parliament the following week called the Constitution Alteration (Aboriginal and Torres Strait Islander Voice) 2023. It proposed the following addition to the Constitution:

Chapter IX—Recognition of Aboriginal and Torres Strait Islander Peoples

129 Aboriginal and Torres Strait Islander Voice

In recognition of Aboriginal and Torres Strait Islander peoples as the First Peoples of Australia:

  (i)   there shall be a body, to be called the Aboriginal and Torres Strait Islander Voice;

  (ii) the Aboriginal and Torres Strait Islander Voice may make representations to the

Parliament and the Executive Government
of the Commonwealth on matters relating to
Aboriginal and Torres Strait Islander peoples;

(iii) the Parliament shall, subject to this
Constitution, have power to make laws with
respect to matters relating to the Aboriginal
and Torres Strait Islander Voice, including its
composition, functions, powers and procedures.

When introducing the Constitution Alteration Bill,
Attorney-General Mark Dreyfus said:

The Constitution Alteration (Aboriginal and Torres
Strait Islander Voice) 2023 is a powerful marker of our
respect for the First Nations peoples of Australia, their
cultures and their elders past and present.

Aboriginal and Torres Strait Islander peoples have
occupied the Australian continent for over 60,000 years
and represent the oldest continuous living cultures in
human history. They have maintained a relationship
with Australia's land, waters and sky since time
immemorial.

Yet Aboriginal and Torres Strait Islander peoples are
not recognised in our Constitution.

This bill is to amend the Australian Constitution to
recognise the First Peoples of Australia by establishing
an Aboriginal and Torres Strait Islander Voice.

It is the first formal step towards holding a
referendum by the end of this year.

It is a form of constitutional recognition that
is practical and substantive – and it is the form
of constitutional recognition supported by the
overwhelming majority of the Aboriginal and Torres
Strait Islander delegates who gathered from all points
under the southern sky in May 2017, on the 50th
anniversary of the 1967 referendum, to endorse the
Uluru Statement from the Heart.[6]

The government's Bill seeks to create the Voice by inserting
a new section 129 into the Constitution. Containing
92 words, the amendment is simple and direct and written
in a style consistent with other clauses in the Constitution.
It strikes a balance between establishing the broad constitutional parameters of the body while leaving key design
features to Parliament. This reflects a choice not to insert
greater detail about the Voice into the Constitution, such
as how its membership should be chosen, its procedures
and the like. Instead, these matters are left to Parliament
to determine from time to time based upon experience and
the expectations of each generation. This enables the Voice
to operate flexibly over the coming years without always
requiring it to conform to the best intentions of 2023.

The Voice will be prefaced by words stating that the
change is '[i]n recognition of Aboriginal and Torres Strait
Islander peoples as the First Peoples of Australia'. This makes
clear why the Constitution is being altered. The Voice is
an act of recognition to ensure that Indigenous peoples are

included in the nation's founding document while affirming their status as the First Peoples of Australia. These words tie the referendum proposal to the concept of recognition, which has been an animating idea in the reconciliation and constitutional change movement for more than two decades.

Clauses (i) and (ii) of the new section 129 entrench the key features of the Voice. If the referendum is passed, these clauses could not be altered by Parliament, and so would give the Voice protection against changing political circumstances. This means that, unless another referendum is held to change section 129, there will be a 'body' (meaning some sort of organisation or entity, rather than an individual) called the Aboriginal and Torres Strait Islander Voice. It will have a constitutionally guaranteed power to make representations to the Parliament and the executive government of the Commonwealth on matters relating to Aboriginal and Torres Strait Islander peoples.

The Voice has a wide scope to make representations. The matter before Parliament or the executive need only relate in some way to Indigenous peoples. There is no requirement that it directly relate to that community or have special significance for them. This means that the Voice could make representations on the specific issues relating to Indigenous peoples, such as matters of culture and heritage, as well as general policy areas, such as taxation and climate change, by talking about how these areas relate to or affect Indigenous peoples. For example, the Voice might make representations about climate change policy by talking about the impact on Torres Strait Islanders of sea level rise.

Clause (ii) of section 129 has been drafted to create a body of Indigenous peoples able to provide advice to Parliament and government without introducing problematic and unintended consequences. The limited scope of the body is made clear by the use of the word 'representations'. This word was carefully chosen to establish that the Voice will speak on behalf of the Indigenous community. The body will provide advice, but does not have a veto, nor can it mandate outcomes. No obligations are placed on other bodies to, for example, wait for the Voice to make a representation. Such obligations might have arisen if, for example, the Constitution said the Voice is to be 'consulted', but this is not what the provision says.

The wording is respectful of Australia's federal arrangements. The Voice is only guaranteed the capacity to make representations to Parliament and the executive government 'of the Commonwealth'. This limits the work of the Voice to these national institutions, while leaving future Parliaments able to increase the remit of the Voice to other bodies and tiers of government. Any extension would be a matter for the people's elected representatives and is not something the Voice itself could initiate. South Australia is well advanced in establishing its own state-based Voice, which might mean that there is no need to empower the national voice to speak to that Parliament.

Clause (iii) of section 129 establishes that Parliament will have the key role of determining how the Voice will operate, including as to its composition, functions, powers and procedures. Parliament's power is not limited to those matters, but is general, extending to making laws 'with respect to matters relating to the Aboriginal and Torres Strait Islander Voice'. This power is expressed in the broadest possible terms and could cover things such as the legal effect of representations by the Voice and the ability of the Voice to speak to other bodies.

The effect of these clauses is to create a new political institution called the Voice with an entrenched power to advise the federal Parliament and executive. The Voice has no legal power beyond the ability to make representations, and so its effectiveness and influence will depend on how well it fulfils its mandate to represent Indigenous peoples across Australia. It is likely to be more effective if it speaks with authority and based on evidence in areas of clear concern to Indigenous peoples. Ultimately, the success of the Voice will be measured in what impact it has upon law-making and policy.

Parliament established a specially convened multi-party committee to examine the Constitution Alteration (Aboriginal and Torres Strait Islander Voice) 2023. The Joint Select Committee on the Aboriginal and Torres Strait Islander Voice Referendum was given six weeks to take sub-missions from the public, hold public hearings and prepare a report.

The Committee delivered its report in mid-May. It found that the submissions and evidence at public hearings supported the introduction of the Voice into the Constitution, and that the government's proposed wording was a safe and sound means of achieving this. The expert evidence on the operation of the Voice did not require changes to be made to the wording of the constitutional change, and so the Committee made only one recommendation: that the Bill 'be passed unamended'.[7] Liberal and National Party members issued dissenting reports consistent with their opposition to the Voice. Liberal members did, however, state that even though they opposed the change they would not stand in the way of Australians having their say on the proposal at a referendum. Parliament then debated the Bill, which was passed by both houses as the necessary final step before being put to the people at a referendum later in 2023.

Myths and misconceptions

Few Australians know much about the Australian Constitution and the words that would bring about the Voice, let alone the implications of this change for our system of government or other parts of the Constitution. This opens up space for misinformation and misunderstanding.

Every referendum throws up a host of horror hypotheticals. This comes from the long-established playbook of those who successfully oppose change. A series of unlikely scenarios that scare voters and make them think twice can generate a strong No vote. The fact that these are often implausible or fanciful makes little difference. The tactic works because few Australians possess sufficient knowledge of the Constitution to distil fact from fiction. Making people confused and frightened can be the most effective way to drum up a No vote.

As we explore in the next chapter, there is nothing in Australian law that punishes people for telling lies about a proposed change to the Constitution. False statements can be made with impunity, with the truth often being the first casualty of a referendum campaign. For example, opponents of a republic in 1999 argued that a Yes vote would lead to the exclusion of Australia from the Commonwealth (and so be unable to compete in the Commonwealth Games), change the flag, cost taxpayers $900 million, give rise to a Hitler-like presidency, and allow claims by Indigenous people to native title across vast areas of Australia. None of these was true, but they nonetheless formed a large part of the public debate.

A similar list of myths and misconceptions is emerging around the Voice. It has been said that the Voice will have a casting vote on matters affecting every Australian, and could spell the end of public holidays such as Australia Day and Anzac Day. The Voice will need to be given a say on whether Australia should go to war and might stop Australia declaring war until the High Court has ruled on the issue. The Voice will mean the end of the federal budget process, with governments unable to introduce their budget into Parliament before the start of the financial year. Others have said that the executive government will be brought to a halt except where it follows the dictates of the Voice, which will be like a new House of Lords. The result will be co-government with Indigenous peoples, amounting to a constitutional 'coup'. There is no substance to these or many other outlandish claims, but equally there is nothing to stop them being made.

Sovereignty under threat?

Some Aboriginal and Torres Strait Islander people have expressed concern that changing the Constitution might frustrate their long-held aspirations for recognition of their sovereignty. Senator Lidia Thorpe, formerly of the Greens, and now an Independent speaking for the 'Blak Sovereign Movement', said that she will oppose the Voice unless it guarantees that First Nations sovereignty is not ceded.

Aboriginal people did not consent to the taking of their lands upon British settlement and have never given up their rights as a sovereign people. Indeed, many Aboriginal people assert their sovereignty to this day. The term 'sovereignty' is a widely used but contested term that can mean different things to different people. At its essence, it refers to the claims of Aboriginal people for recognition of their laws and their right to govern their own affairs.

In the *Mabo* case of 1992, the High Court recognised the native title rights of Aboriginal and Torres Strait Islander peoples. However, in later cases, the Court made it clear that this does not amount to recognition of their sovereignty. It said that native title is recognised by Australian law only because it can be accommodated within the common law brought to Australia by the British settlers in 1788. As a result, Australian courts do not recognise that Aboriginal and Torres Strait Islander peoples possess a sovereign law-making power.

Underlying the High Court's reasoning is the view that the sovereignty of Australia's First Peoples was displaced by British settlement and the introduction of their law. This was brought about by the assertion by the British of their sovereignty over the Australian continent. All of this occurred before the Australian Constitution came into force in 1901. That document created a new nation upon a continent that the British already regarded as theirs.

This represents the position under Australian law, of which the Constitution is the ultimate expression. It does not affect how Aboriginal people view their own sovereignty. As a result, it does not prevent them from asserting their own independence and the continuing validity of their laws and customs.

The Voice referendum will not compromise these claims, nor challenge the idea that Indigenous peoples never ceded their rights. This issue was examined by the Constitutional Expert Group advising the Albanese government on the referendum. The Expert Group were unanimous in answering a question about the extinguishment of Indigenous sovereignty with an emphatic 'no'. They concluded that the referendum will 'not affect the sovereignty of any group or body'.[8]

This is borne out by the wording of the constitutional change, which says nothing at all about sovereignty. It would only create a new body of Indigenous peoples able to make representations to Parliament and government about the issues affecting them. The amendment does not speak to the colonisation of Australia, nor issues like native title or self-determination. Bringing the Constitution into force in 1901 and the passage of the 1967 referendum did not undermine Indigenous sovereignty. Nor would the Voice referendum. People can be confident that the status quo will be unaffected.

The right place to advance the sovereignty debate is instead through a treaty process. Treaties are used across the world to negotiate coexistence between First Peoples and those who colonised their lands. They are a means of moving forward together by acknowledging the prior history and sovereignty of the peoples upon whose lands the nation is founded. Treaties put in place practical measures to improve lives, enable economic empowerment and recognise decision-making by local communities. Negotiating these measures, and then implementing them, is itself a powerful assertion of Indigenous sovereignty.

The Uluru Statement from the Heart makes it clear that Aboriginal people never ceded their sovereignty. It says:

> Our Aboriginal and Torres Strait Islander tribes were the first sovereign Nations of the Australian continent and its adjacent islands, and possessed it under our own laws and customs. This our ancestors did, according to the reckoning of our culture, from the Creation, according to the common law from 'time immemorial', and according to science more than 60,000 years ago.

> This sovereignty is *a spiritual notion: the ancestral tie between the land, or 'mother nature', and the Aboriginal and Torres Strait Islander peoples who were born therefrom, remain attached thereto, and must one day return thither to be united with our ancestors. This link is the basis of the ownership of the soil, or better, of sovereignty.* It has never been ceded or extinguished, and co-exists with the sovereignty of the Crown.

> How could it be otherwise? That peoples possessed a land for sixty millennia and this sacred link disappears from world history in merely the last two hundred years?

> With substantive constitutional change and structural
> reform, we believe this ancient sovereignty can
> shine through as a fuller expression of Australia's
> nationhood.[9]

These words demonstrate that sovereignty forms the basis
for the Uluru Statement and that the reforms set out in the
Statement, including the Voice, are designed to express that
sovereignty rather than to deny it.

A third chamber of Parliament?

In the days after the Uluru Convention, Deputy Prime
Minister Barnaby Joyce labelled the Voice a 'new chamber'
of Parliament. A few months later, Prime Minister
Malcolm Turnbull rejected the Voice by describing it as
a 'third chamber' of Parliament and so incompatible with
Australia's parliamentary system.

Joyce later admitted he may have been mistaken, saying,
'if I got it wrong, I apologise'. Others have also taken issue
with the description, including the Joint Select Committee,
chaired by Pat Dodson and Julian Leeser, and the Final
Report of the Referendum Council.

The Voice is not a chamber of Parliament. It would
have no law-making functions. It could not introduce, vote
on, or reject legislation. It would, as a result, not fetter the
power of Parliament and is consistent with the notion of
parliamentary supremacy. It has none of the features of a
chamber of Parliament. As constitutional lawyer Anne
Twomey has pointed out, the Voice is not 'a constituent part

of the body that makes laws. Its role would be to give a voice to Indigenous views that could be heard within the Parliament'.[10]

The wording of the constitutional change confirms this. It does not grant the Voice a veto over Parliament or government. The words only permit the Voice to 'make representations' to these bodies. The word 'representations' was carefully chosen to limit the body to an advisory role. There is no basis upon which making 'representations' can amount to having a veto or the final say.

Special rights?

It has been suggested that the Voice would create special rights for Indigenous people. This is not supported by the wording of the change. No extra rights or entitlements would be conferred, only a new opportunity for Aboriginal and Torres Strait Islander peoples to have their voice heard in Parliament and government on matters that affect them.

The Voice is consistent with the principles set out in the United Nations Declaration on the Rights of Indigenous Peoples. Article 18 states that Indigenous peoples must be able to 'participate in decision-making in matters which would affect their rights, through representatives chosen by themselves in accordance with their own procedures'. The Voice embodies the goal of this Article by giving Indigenous people the ability to speak about their rights and to assert them. It is then up to Parliament and the executive government as to what weight it gives these representations.

Recognition and race

One concern that goes to the core of the Voice referendum is that inserting references to Aboriginal and Torres Strait Islander peoples into the Constitution perpetuates race-based distinctions. It has been suggested that the Voice might even introduce racial division in Australia.

Mentioning a group of people in the Constitution is not unusual. The document already refers to the people of the Commonwealth and of the particular states on numerous occasions. It does so because the Constitution needs to identify particular peoples for purposes such as voting. State populations are also mentioned in the preamble to the British Act that brought about the Australian Constitution (except for the people of Western Australia, who are not mentioned because they only agreed to join the Federation after the preamble had been drafted).

Referring to Aboriginal people in the Constitution would be consistent with this. Indigenous people would not be referred to in creating the Voice because of an unscientific resort to race. Instead, they would be recognised due to their unique status as the original inhabitants and first peoples of the Australian continent. The Constitution would recognise them because they have a historical and cultural connection to the land upon which the nation has been founded.

Other nations adopt a like approach in rejecting the concept of racial discrimination while making mention of their Indigenous peoples. For example, section 35 of the Canadian Constitution refers to Indigenous peoples by way of recognising and affirming their 'existing aboriginal and treaty rights'.[11] Similarly, the Indigenous peoples of Scandinavia, the Sami, are recognised in the constitutions of Norway and Finland. The 1814 *Constitution of the Kingdom of Norway* states in article 108: 'The authorities of the state shall create conditions enabling the Sami people to preserve and develop its language, culture and way of life'.[12] Section 17 of the 1999 *Constitution of Finland* provides: 'The Sami, as an indigenous people … have the right to maintain and develop their own language and culture'.[13] Such constitutions reflect the unique status of Indigenous peoples in the nation.

It is important to consider how this relates to the race power. That power in section 51(xxvi) of the Constitution allows federal legislation to be passed for 'the people of any race for whom it is deemed necessary to make special laws' and has only ever been used to make laws for Aboriginal and Torres Strait Islander peoples. At the Regional Dialogues and Uluru, there was no appetite for removing or amending this provision in the Constitution. Rather, the Voice would 'monitor' the Commonwealth's use of this provision and section 122, the 'territories power'. This would enable use of these powers to be contested and the views of Indigenous people to be heard in the debate. The Voice would thus fill an important function as a counterweight to the race power without establishing race-based distinctions.

Will government decision-making grind to a halt?

People have suggested that the Voice could produce mountains of expensive litigation in the High Court that will slow down and even block decision-making by the executive government. It has been argued that the Voice could undermine decision-making by the Reserve Bank and the appointment of High Court judges, and prevent federal governments delivering budgets in a timely fashion.

The wording of the change does not support this, though we can expect the courts will play a limited role in the operation of the Voice. It is a basic element of the rule of law that every government institution is subject to judicial scrutiny. No person, and no body, is above the law. Every constitutional provision, and indeed every law, raises the prospect of oversight by the courts. Those who exercise public power must be held in check by the possibility of review by an independent judge.

The High Court might be called upon to keep the Voice within its constitutional limits. The Voice will be able to make representations to Parliament and government on matters relating to Aboriginal and Torres Strait Islander peoples. The Voice might be challenged in court if it operates outside these parameters. For example, someone might bring an injunction to stop the Voice from making representations on matters that do not relate to Indigenous peoples. The Voice could also be prevented from making representations to bodies, such as the United Nations, unless this has been authorised by Parliament. Judicial oversight provides the community with confidence that the system can ensure the Voice operates as set out in the Constitution.

What happens, though, if Parliament or the executive refuses to listen to a representation by the Voice, perhaps by refusing to read or even receive its advice? In the case of parliamentarians, there is little or no prospect of a successful

High Court challenge. The Court has said repeatedly over the course of more than a century that it will not intervene in the internal workings of Parliament. This is a key aspect of the separation of powers in Australia, and is not something the Voice would change. It means that Parliament could make laws without listening to the Voice should it so wish.

Courts are more likely to scrutinise the work of ministers and other public officials. We expect that people who exercise public power on behalf of the community will make fair decisions following a sound process. This includes taking into account information relevant to making the decision. If a public official fails to consider important information of this kind, courts routinely direct that person to go back and make the decision again, taking into account the information that was missed. Courts do not direct what the decision should be, only that it is properly made.

The upshot is that ministers who receive a representation from the Voice may need to read and consider that representation when they make a decision. For example, if a minister is considering whether to permit a development on the land of an Indigenous community, and the Voice had made representations about whether this is a sound idea and the impact on the community, the minister should take this into account. If the minister refused to even receive advice from the Voice, someone might go to court to ask the minister to remake the decision with the benefit of all the relevant information. Even then, court cases of this kind can be avoided with proper procedures within government, like those that already operate in areas such as immigration and social security, to ensure that decisions are well and fairly made.

This is the system working as it should. The rule of law and independent oversight by judges should apply to the Voice as they do to every other government body. The Voice must operate within its limits, and representations by the Voice should be taken into account when making decisions that affect Indigenous people. This does not give the final say to the Voice. It only means that ministers and public officials should listen to what the Voice has to say.

This was confirmed in advice provided to the government by its top legal officer, Solicitor-General Stephen Donaghue KC, in April 2023. He concluded that the Voice would not generate high volumes of litigation, nor cause problems for government processes. He also concluded that: 'in my opinion proposed s 129 is not just compatible with the system of representative and responsible government prescribed by the Constitution, but an enhancement of that system'.[14]

8

THE VOICE REFERENDUM

There is only one way to change the Constitution: it must be supported by the people voting at a referendum. Australia's referendum record provides good and bad news for those who support the Voice.

The good news is that Australians overwhelmingly voted Yes at the last referendum held on Indigenous issues. They did so in 1967 when over 90 per cent of voters granted the federal Parliament power to make laws for Aboriginal people and removed a prohibition on Aboriginal people being counted in the national population. The bad news is that the 1967 poll is exceptional. The larger picture shows a landscape littered with referendum failures. Australians have passed very few proposals at a referendum and none in recent decades.

Changing the Constitution requires high levels of popular support across the nation. This was certainly true of the 1967 referendum and will be true for a constitutional Voice.

How does a referendum work?

Section 128 of the Constitution provides the only way to alter the document (the text of this clause is set out in appendix 3 of this book: see pages 195–96). It sets out two steps that require the coming together of Australia's elected federal representatives and the community at large.

First, a 'proposed law' for changing the text of the Constitution must be passed by the federal Parliament. The normal method is for the proposal to win the support of an absolute majority of both Houses. However, if one House fails to pass it, a special procedure may be invoked whereby the proposal can instead be passed twice by an absolute majority of the members of a single House.

Second, between two and six months after the proposed law has been approved by Parliament, it must be submitted to the people at a referendum. Any person able to vote in federal elections can take part. The proposal must achieve a double majority:

- a majority of people across the nation must vote Yes; and
- a majority of the people in a majority of the states (that is, in at least four out of six states) must vote Yes.

People living in the Australian Capital Territory and the Northern Territory do not get the same vote as other Australians. This is because their vote is only counted in calculating the first majority, and not the second.

The mechanics of holding a referendum are set down in a federal law, the *Referendum (Machinery Provisions) Act 1984*. Voters are informed about the proposal by the Electoral Commissioner sending each household a Yes/No pamphlet at least two weeks before voting day showing the proposed amendment to the Constitution, with arguments for and against the proposal of not more than 2000 words each. These for and against arguments are authorised by members of Parliament on each side of the debate.

The Yes/No pamphlet was introduced in 1912 by the Fisher Labor government, which had been stung by the heavy defeat of its 1911 referendum proposals. The government believed it lost the referendum because of an exaggerated No campaign and hoped the pamphlet would inject rationality into the debate. Attorney-General William Hughes envisaged the case for either side being put in an 'impersonal, reasonable and judicial way', and appealing to 'reason rather than to the emotions and party sentiments'.[1] Prime Minister Andrew Fisher was optimistic about the pamphlet, remarking: 'I have no doubt at all that the case will be put from both sides impersonally and free from any suggestion of bias or misleading on the one side or the other'.[2]

The first referendum to use the pamphlet was in 1913 when the Fisher Labor government put six proposals to the people to increase Commonwealth power over trade and commerce, corporations, industrial matters, railways, trusts and monopolies. Government members drafted the Yes case in the pamphlet to appeal to reason and the responsibility of citizens to serve the common good. The

EVERYTHING YOU NEED TO KNOW ABOUT THE VOICE

No case went for the jugular. It urged people to vote no 'against the rash, reckless and unreasonable wrecking of the Federal Constitution'. It said a Yes vote would 'pave the way for the introduction and adoption of ... Socialism' and that a 'Socialistic Government ... would pose and preside as our Dictator, while living upon the captured earnings and savings of the whole people, until finally the bubble project bursting plunges all concerned into inevitable disaster'.[3] The No case won the day, with all six proposals defeated.

The 1913 referendum set the scene for future Yes/No pamphlets containing unrestrained language and mis-information. Many wild claims have been made in the hope of appealing to emotion, rather than reason. Hyperbole and falsehood have often proven effective techniques for influencing voters who have little knowledge of how the Constitution works and so cannot separate fact from fiction.

The Albanese Labor government sought to drop the Yes/No pamphlet for the 2023 referendum on the Voice. It said that the pamphlet was no longer needed to enable the community to hear the views of their elected representatives. A written pamphlet may have been required in 1912 before the advent of radio and television in Australia, let alone the internet and social media, whereas today politicians have many opportunities to get their point across. However, the proposal to do away with the pamphlet for the Voice referendum was staunchly opposed by the Opposition and the idea was dropped.

The *Referendum (Machinery Provisions) Act* does not require the pamphlet or other campaigning material to be truthful. At best, it makes it an offence to print, publish or distribute any information likely to mislead or deceive electors *in relation to the casting of a vote at the referendum*. This applies to statements affecting the casting of a person's ballot (for example, to a statement misleading people as to how to mark their paper to cast a valid vote). It does not apply to statements intended to influence whether people vote Yes or No. There is no legal requirement to avoid misleading people about the referendum proposal. This leaves open the possibility that the Yes and No cases can lie or mislead voters to influence the result. Indeed, some of the most influential arguments put at past referendums have had no basis in fact.

The Act sets out who must vote at the referendum. It says that 'it is the duty of every elector to vote at a referendum', with a penalty of up to $50 for failing to do so. In practice, this means that attending and having your name marked off is compulsory, but because the ballot is secret no one can tell whether someone has actually voted. Voting takes place in the same way as for a general election. People mark their voting paper in secret in a booth and place their completed vote in a ballot box.

The law stops the Commonwealth from spending taxpayer dollars on the referendum campaign. The *Referendum (Machinery Provisions) Act* says that the 'Commonwealth shall not expend money in respect of the presentation of the argument in favour of, or the argument against' a proposal to change the Constitution, except for funding:

- the preparation, printing, posting and translation of the official pamphlets containing the Yes and No cases (including in various languages, and in forms appropriate for the visually impaired);
- the Australian Electoral Commission to provide information relating to the proposal or its effect; and
- the salaries and allowances of members of Parliament (and their staff) and of the public service.

Amendments made to the law in preparation of the Voice referendum in 2023 further provided that the Commonwealth can spend money 'in relation to neutral public civics education and awareness activities', which 'must not address the arguments for or against a proposed law for the alteration of the Constitution'.

Restrictions on referendum expenditure only apply to the Commonwealth. State and local governments, political parties and major interest groups have no restriction on what they can spend. Changes introduced to the Voice referendum do, however, introduce new restrictions on expenditure from outside Australia. Other nations, foreign entities and individuals cannot donate more than $100 to a referendum campaign, are prevented from authorising advertisements to influence how people vote at the referendum and cannot spend more than a $1000 on campaigning in the referendum.

Changes introduced in 2023 also mean that Australian referendum campaigners must disclose expenditure and donations over the disclosure threshold (currently $15 200). This information is made public by the Australian Electoral Commission up to 24 weeks after voting day in the referendum. No provision is made for real-time disclosure, or indeed any other means by which voters can be told prior to the day of the ballot who has funded the Yes and No cases.

Holding a national vote is an expensive and challenging logistical exercise. All up, the federal Parliament has approved $364.6 million over three years to deliver the referendum to recognise Aboriginal and Torres Strait peoples in the Constitution through the Voice. This includes:

- $336.6 million for the Australian Electoral Commission to deliver the referendum, including $10.6 million to produce the Yes/No pamphlet for all Australian households;
- $12.0 million for the National Indigenous Australians Agency and the Museum of Australian Democracy for neutral public civics education and awareness activities;
- $10.5 million to the Department of Health and Aged Care to increase mental health supports for First Nations people during the period of the referendum; and
- $5.5 million to the National Indigenous Australians Agency for consultation, policy and delivery connected to holding the referendum.

Funding of $20 million was also provided to progress regional Voice arrangements to complement the referendum.[4]

Finally, the Act provides an awkward format for the question put to voters. The ballot paper must set out the short title of the proposed law, as approved by Parliament, and then ask whether the voter approves the law. They indicate this by writing Yes or No. This means that in 2023, Australians will be asked the following question:

A Proposed Law: to alter the Constitution to recognise the First Peoples of Australia by establishing an Aboriginal and Torres Strait Islander Voice.

Do you approve this proposed alteration?

The referendum record

Since Federation in 1901, 44 referendum proposals have been put to the Australian people. Only eight have succeeded, less than one in five. No referendum has been passed by the people since 1977 when Australians voted, among other things, to set a retirement age of 70 years for High Court judges. As at 2023, 46 years have passed since Australia changed its Constitution. This is by far the longest period that Australia has gone without amending its founding document.

The reasons for the low success rate of referendums are not always easy to identify. It might be thought that referendums are less likely to succeed when held concurrently with a federal election, yet the evidence does not bear this out. Twenty-two of the 44 referendums have been held on election day, with the other half held mid-term. The success rate is identical, with four referendums passed in each case. However, more than 75 years have passed since the last successful election-day referendum in 1946.

It is possible to single out particular states as willing or unwilling to vote Yes. Tasmania has rejected more referendums than any other state (34 out of 44), whereas Western Australia is the only state to have voted Yes in a majority of referendums (23 out of 44). Some of the state voting patterns have changed over time. For example, New South Wales voted against all but three of the 19 proposals put until 1946, but since then has voted for a majority of the proposed changes (14 out of 25), the only state to do so. On the other hand, Western Australia voted Yes to all of the first 13 referendums, while Queensland voted Yes to 15 of the first 17. Yet, neither Western Australia nor Queensland, South Australia or Tasmania has supported any referendum since 1977.

The record also reflects the nature of the proposal put to the people. Unsurprisingly, given that referendums can only be initiated by the federal Parliament, most proposals (24 out of 44) have sought to expand Commonwealth power, including by adding new legislative powers to section 51 of the Constitution over subjects such as industrial relations, employment, monopolies, trusts, essential services, the marketing of primary products, social services, communism, and rents and prices. Australians have overwhelmingly rejected such proposals, with only three succeeding.

The political party in government putting the referendum also plays a part in explaining the figures. The Australian Labor Party has not succeeded at a referendum since 1946. That referendum, which granted the federal Parliament power over social services such as maternity allowances and unemployment benefits, represents the only time, in 25 attempts, that a Labor government has convinced the Australian people to vote Yes. This success rate of 4 per cent contrasts unfavourably with that of Australia's non-Labor governments. Seven of 19 non-Labor proposals (37 per cent) have been passed, reflecting in part

Referendums to change the Australian Constitution

Shading indicates a successful referendum

Year	Proposal	Government submitting	States approving	National Yes Vote (%)
1906	Senate elections	Protectionist	6	82.65
1910	Finance	Fusion	3 (Qld, WA, Tas)	49.04
	State debts	Fusion	5 (all except NSW)	54.95
1911	Legislative powers	ALP	1 (WA)	39.42
	Monopolies	ALP	1 (WA)	39.89
1913	Trade and commerce	ALP	3 (Qld, WA, SA)	49.38
	Corporations	ALP	3 (Qld, WA, SA)	49.33
	Industrial matters	ALP	3 (Qld, WA, SA)	49.33
	Railway disputes	ALP	3 (Qld, WA, SA)	49.13
	Trusts	ALP	3 (Qld, WA, SA)	49.78
	Nationalisation of monopolies	ALP	3 (Qld, WA, SA)	49.33
1919	Legislative powers	Nationalist	3 (Vic, Qld, WA)	49.65
	Nationalisation of monopolies	Nationalist	3 (Vic, Qld, WA)	48.64
1926	Industry and commerce	Nat–CP	2 (NSW, Qld)	43.50
	Essential services	Nat–CP	2 (NSW, Qld)	42.80
1928	State debts	Nat–CP	6	74.30
1937	Aviation	UAP	2 (Vic, Qld)	53.56
	Marketing	UAP	0	36.26
1944	Post-war reconstruction and democratic rights	ALP	2 (WA, SA)	45.99
1946	Social services	ALP	6	54.39
	Organised marketing	ALP	3 (NSW, Vic, WA)	50.57
	Industrial employment	ALP	3 (NSW, Vic, WA)	50.30

Year	Proposal	Government submitting	States approving	National Yes Vote (%)
1948	Rents and prices	ALP	0	40.66
1951	Communism	Lib–CP	3 (Qld, WA, Tas)	49.44
1967	Parliament	Lib–CP	1 (NSW)	40.25
	Aboriginals	Lib–CP	6	90.77
1973	Prices	ALP	0	43.81
	Incomes	ALP	0	34.42
1974	Simultaneous elections	ALP	1 (NSW)	48.30
	Mode of altering the Constitution	ALP	1 (NSW)	47.99
	Democratic elections	ALP	1 (NSW)	47.20
	Local government bodies	ALP	1 (NSW)	46.85
1977	Simultaneous elections	Lib–NP	3 (NSW, Vic, SA)	62.22
	Senate casual vacancies	Lib–NP	6	73.32
	Referendums	Lib–NP	6	77.72
	Retirement of judges	Lib–NP	6	80.10
1984	Terms of senators	ALP	2 (NSW, Vic)	50.64
	Interchange of powers	ALP	0	47.06
1988	Parliamentary terms	ALP	0	32.92
	Fair elections	ALP	0	37.60
	Local government	ALP	0	33.62
	Rights and freedoms	ALP	0	30.79
1999	Establishment of republic	Lib–NP	0	45.13
	Preamble to Constitution	Lib–NP	0	39.34

Labor's greater willingness to support referendum proposals from opposition.

It is sometimes suggested that a difficulty arises from the 'majority of States' requirement in section 128; that is, that a majority of voters in a majority of the states must support the proposal. However, only in three instances – two ballots in 1946 and one in 1977 – would this have made any difference. In fact, in every case where a Yes vote prevailed, with the exception of a 1910 referendum, the national majority was accompanied by a Yes vote in every state.

The failure to achieve bipartisanship has also been identified as a common reason for referendum failure in Australia. To date, no referendum has succeeded without the support of both of Australia's major parties. A lack of bipartisanship has been a feature of failed referendums put by the Australian Labor Party. Of the 25 proposals it has put to the Australian people, only one has attracted the support of the opposition. That also happens to be the only occasion, in 1946, on which the people passed a proposal put by Labor.

The loss of bipartisanship in the 2023 Voice referendum increases the order of difficulty markedly. It is wrong, though, to see history as determining the fate of this referendum. It is nearly a quarter century since Australia's last referendum, and popular allegiance to the major political parties has weakened greatly, meaning that bipartisanship may not be as essential to referendum success as it has proved to be in the past.

It is also significant that the Voice has a strong grassroots base. Referendum after referendum has failed in Australia because it has been driven by politicians. The Voice is instead embedded in the aspirations of our first peoples, and has attracted support from across the community and civil society. The last time a referendum was held on Indigenous issues it was also supported by a large community base. That was the 1967 referendum put to the people by Liberal Prime Minister Harold Holt. It achieved Australia's greatest ever referendum success with over 90 per cent of the community voting Yes. Such a result is out of reach this time around, but it is still possible for the referendum on the Voice to be won without the support of both of Australia's major political parties.

Just as deadly as partisan opposition to the fate of past referendums is the perception that a constitutional reform is a 'politicians' proposal' lacking popular ownership. From proposals which have been felled by the cry of 'no more politicians', to the republic referendum in 1999, which was killed off by the claim that it was the 'politicians' republic', Australians have consistently voted No when they believe a proposal is motivated by politicians' self-interest. This reflects a well-known undercurrent of distrust by Australians of their elected representatives.

The design of the referendum process worsens this problem. Politicians, and only politicians, can initiate constitutional reform through the federal Parliament. This renders every proposal at risk of being perceived as self-serving, especially of those interests aligned with the Commonwealth.

Popular ownership is difficult to achieve. It cuts against the grain of how Australian politics normally works, where politicians are only too ready to claim ownership of reforms and successes. Popular ownership was achieved in the 1967 referendum because it emerged out of a long-running people's movement.

On that occasion, the referendum was held not because the prime minister of the day saw it as a priority, but as a response to a popular demand for change that had been building for decades.

The Voice is also generating strong community backing and involvement. At the Regional Dialogues and at the Uluru National Convention, the consensus decision reached – for Voice, Treaty, Truth – was important precisely because there was a sense of popular ownership of the decision among Indigenous peoples. This now needs to be realised in the broader Australian community to give the referendum the best chance of success.

Another challenge to achieving referendum success is low levels of knowledge in the community about the Constitution. Surveys of the Australian public show a disturbing lack of knowledge about their system of government. Many Australians know little of even the most basic aspects of government. This is often a reflection of citizens being disengaged from many aspects of their democracy. The problem has been demonstrated over many years.

A 1987 survey for the Constitutional Commission found that almost half the population did not realise Australia has a Constitution, with the figure being nearly 70 per cent of Australians aged between 18 and 24. In 2015, a survey showed that only 65 per cent of the population knew that Australia had a Constitution. Other reports have shown that only one in five people had some understanding of what the Constitution contained, while more than a quarter named the Supreme Court, not the High Court, as the 'top' court in Australia. Finally, in 2006, Amnesty International Australia commissioned a nationwide poll of 1001 voters by Roy Morgan Research, in which, remarkably, 61 per cent said they thought Australia has a national Bill of Rights.

The results suggest that many Australians know more about the United States system of government than our own, perhaps in part because of the prevalence of US popular culture. This can produce confusion about how the Australian system works, as many people assume that the Australian system is the same as that of the United States.

These problems can be telling during a referendum campaign. A lack of knowledge, or false knowledge, on the part of the voter, can translate into a misunderstanding of a proposal, a potential to be manipulated by the Yes or No cases, and even an unwillingness to consider change on the basis that 'don't know, vote No' is the best policy. Misunderstanding the Constitution can mean that people can cast a Yes or No vote to a proposal in a way that does not reflect their real intentions. A person may vote No out of a mistaken concern about the impact of the proposal, even if they would have supported the proposal had they fully understood it.

Overall, the record shows that when voters do not understand or have no opinion on a proposal, they tend to vote No. Polls from the 1999 referendum showed that many people had not read the official pamphlet distributed by the Commonwealth to explain the proposals, and that people who had not read the pamphlet were far more likely to vote No. Polling in the lead-up to the 1967, 1977 and 1988 referendums also suggested that those who did not know which way they would vote shortly before the referendum swung heavily into the No column on the day of the vote.

The coming vote

Australia's long record of failed attempts at constitutional reform does not mean that winning a referendum today is 'mission impossible'. Instead, it only shows that a referendum is more likely to fail whenever the nation's major political parties disagree, or when poor management by our leaders means that the Australian people feel left out or confused about what is being changed. People will also vote No to a proposal that is dangerous or has been poorly thought out.

Changing Australia's Constitution to create a Voice to Parliament is achievable. If nothing else, we should not forget the 1967 referendum. Not only was that referendum passed, the Yes vote reached a record high in securing over 90 per cent support from the Australian people. That momentous national vote shows what is possible if the right proposal to change the Constitution is put to the Australian people in the right way.

This referendum is about Australia continuing its journey of coming to terms with a past in which Aboriginal people were discriminated against and denied basic freedoms. The Voice offers the opportunity to recast the Australian Constitution to provide for a more positive future in which the Aboriginal and Torres Strait Islander history of this

continent is recognised. As the Uluru Statement from the
Heart says, in 1967, Aboriginal and Torres Strait Islander
people 'were counted, in 2017 we seek to be heard'.

APPENDIX 1

ULURU STATEMENT FROM THE HEART

We, gathered at the 2017 National Constitutional Convention, coming from all points of the southern sky, make this statement from the heart:

Our Aboriginal and Torres Strait Islander tribes were the first sovereign Nations of the Australian continent and its adjacent islands, and possessed it under our own laws and customs. This our ancestors did, according to the reckoning of our culture, from the Creation, according to the common law from 'time immemorial', and according to science more than 60 000 years ago.

This sovereignty is *a spiritual notion: the ancestral tie between the land, or 'mother nature', and the Aboriginal and Torres Strait Islander peoples who were born therefrom, remain attached thereto, and must one day return thither to be united with our ancestors. This link is the basis of the ownership of the soil, or better, of sovereignty.* It has never been ceded or extinguished, and co-exists with the sovereignty of the Crown.

How could it be otherwise? That peoples possessed a land for sixty millennia and this sacred link disappears from world history in merely the last two hundred years?

With substantive constitutional change and structural reform, we believe this ancient sovereignty can shine through as a fuller expression of Australia's nationhood.

Proportionally, we are the most incarcerated people on the planet. We are not an innately criminal people. Our children are aliened from their families at unprecedented rates. This cannot be because we have no love for them. And our youth languish in detention in obscene numbers. They should be our hope for the future.

These dimensions of our crisis tell plainly the structural nature of our problem. This is *the torment of our powerlessness.*

We seek constitutional reforms to empower our people and take *a rightful place* in our own country. When we have power over our destiny our children will flourish. They will walk in two worlds and their culture will be a gift to their country.

We call for the establishment of a First Nations Voice enshrined in the Constitution.

Makarrata is the culmination of our agenda: *the coming together after a struggle.* It captures our aspirations for a fair and truthful relationship with the people of Australia and a better future for our children based on justice and self-determination.

We seek a Makarrata Commission to supervise a process of agreement-making between governments and First Nations and truth-telling about our history.

In 1967 we were counted, in 2017 we seek to be heard. We leave base camp and start our trek across this vast country. We invite you to walk with us in a movement of the Australian people for a better future.

APPENDIX 2

PROPOSED AMENDMENT TO THE AUSTRALIAN CONSTITUTION

Chapter IX—Recognition of Aboriginal and Torres Strait Islander Peoples

129. Aboriginal and Torres Strait Islander Voice

In recognition of Aboriginal and Torres Strait Islander peoples as the First Peoples of Australia:

(i) there shall be a body, to be called the Aboriginal and Torres Strait Islander Voice;

(ii) the Aboriginal and Torres Strait Islander Voice may make representations to the Parliament and the Executive Government of the Commonwealth on matters relating to Aboriginal and Torres Strait Islander peoples;

(iii) the Parliament shall, subject to this Constitution, have power to make laws with respect to matters relating to the Aboriginal and Torres Strait Islander Voice, including its composition, functions, powers and procedures.

APPENDIX 3

SECTION 128 OF THE AUSTRALIAN CONSTITUTION

128. Mode of altering the Constitution

This Constitution shall not be altered except in the following manner:

The proposed law for the alteration thereof must be passed by an absolute majority of each House of the Parliament, and not less than two nor more than six months after its passage through both Houses the proposed law shall be submitted in each State and Territory to the electors qualified to vote for the election of members of the House of Representatives.

But if either House passes any such proposed law by an absolute majority, and the other House rejects or fails to pass it, or passes it with any amendment to which the first-mentioned House will not agree, and if after an interval of three months the first-mentioned House in the same or the next session again passes the proposed law by an absolute majority with or without any amendment which has been made or agreed to by the other House, and such other House rejects or fails to pass it or passes it with any amendment to which the first-mentioned House will not agree, the Governor-General may submit the proposed law as last proposed by the first-mentioned House, and either with or without any amendments subsequently agreed to by both Houses, to the electors in each State and Territory qualified to vote for the election of the House of Representatives.

When a proposed law is submitted to the electors the vote shall be taken in such manner as the Parliament pre-scribes. But until the qualification of electors of members of the House of Representatives becomes uniform throughout the Commonwealth, only one-half the electors voting for and against the proposed law shall be counted in any State in which adult suffrage prevails.

And if in a majority of the States a majority of the electors voting approve the proposed law, and if a majority of all the electors voting also approve the proposed law, it shall be presented to the Governor-General for the Queen's assent.

No alteration diminishing the proportionate represen-tation of any State in either House of the Parliament, or the minimum number of representatives of a State in the House of Representatives, or increasing, diminishing, or otherwise altering the limits of the State, or in any manner affecting the provisions of the Constitution in relation thereto, shall become law unless the majority of the electors voting in that State approve the proposed law.

In this section, 'Territory' means any territory referred to in section one hundred and twenty-two of this Constitution in respect of which there is in force a law allowing its representation in the House of Representatives.

ACKNOWLEDGMENTS

The authors acknowledge those people who assisted with their earlier works *Everything You Need to Know about the Referendum to Recognise Indigenous Australians* and *Everything You Need to Know about the Uluru Statement from the Heart*. This book is developed from those publications.

NOTES

Introduction

1   Royal Australian and New Zealand College of Psychiatrists, 'Mental Health Benefits in Constitutional Recognition of Indigenous Australians', Media Release, 25 May 2011.

1   Making the Constitution

1   Bill Gammage, *The Biggest Estate on Earth: How Aborigines Made Australia*, Allen & Unwin, Sydney, 2011, p. 2.

2   Secret Instructions from Lord Morton to Lieutenant James Cook, 30 July 1768.

3   Raymond Evans, *A History of Queensland*, Cambridge University Press, Melbourne, 2007, p. 18.

4   Draught Instructions from Lord Sydney to Governor Phillip, 25 April 1787.

5   Expert Panel on Constitutional Recognition of Indigenous Australians, *Recognising Aboriginal and Torres Strait Islander Peoples in the Constitution: Report of the Expert Panel*, Report, 16 January 2012, pp. 1–3.

6   Russel Ward, *Concise History of Australia*, University of Queensland Press, Brisbane (first published 1965), 1992, p. 56.

7   Garth Nettheim et al., *Indigenous Legal Issues*, 4th edition, Thomson Reuters, Sydney, 2009, p. 21.

8   David Neal, *The Rule of Law in a Penal Colony: Law and Power in Early New South Wales*, Cambridge University Press, Melbourne, 1991, p. 17.

9   Sir Henry Parkes, 'Tenterfield Oration', Speech delivered at the Tenterfield School of Arts, 24 October 1889.

10   Margaret Jolly, *Family and Gender in the Pacific: Domestic Contradictions and the Colonial Impact*, Cambridge University Press, Melbourne, 1989, p. 239.

11   *Official Record of the Debates of the Australasian Federal Convention: 1891–1898* (Convention Debates), Melbourne, 3 March 1898, p. 1784 (John Quick). Dr Quick also refers to 'people of any undesirable race or of undesirable antecedents': Convention Debates, Melbourne, 2 March 1898, p. 1752.

12   *Commonwealth of Australia Constitution Act 1900* (Imp) 63 & 64 Vict, preamble.

13   Australian Constitution section 127, as repealed by *Constitution Alteration (Aboriginals) 1967* (Cth) section 3.

14 *Official Record of the Debates of the Australasian Federal Convention: 1891–1898*, Melbourne, 8 February 1898, p. 713 (Edmund Barton).

15 Australian Constitution section 51(xxvi), later amended by *Constitution Alteration (Aboriginals) 1967* (Cth) section 2.

16 Harrison Moore, *The Constitution of the Commonwealth of Australia*, 2nd edition, Maxwell, Melbourne, 1910, p. 464.

17 *Official Record of the Debates of the National Australasian Convention*, Sydney (2 March – 9 April 1891), 8 April 1891, p. 703 (Sir Samuel Griffith).

18 *Official Record of the Debates of the Australasian Federal Convention: 1891–1898*, Melbourne, 27 January 1898, pp. 228–29 (Edmund Barton).

19 John Quick and Robert Garran, *The Annotated Constitution of the Australian Commonwealth*, Angus & Robertson, Sydney, 1901, p. 622.

20 *Official Record of the Debates of the Australasian Federal Convention: 1891–1898*, Melbourne, 28 January 1898, p. 250 (Josiah Symon).

21 John Quick and Robert Garran, *The Annotated Constitution of the Australian Commonwealth*, Angus & Robertson, Sydney, 1901, p. 623.

22 *Official Record of the Debates of the Australasian Federal Convention: 1891–1898*, Melbourne, 27 January 1898, p. 240 (Sir John Forrest).

23 *Official Record of the Debates of the Australasian Federal Convention: 1891–1898*, Melbourne, 8 February 1898, pp. 665–66 (Sir John Forrest).

24 *Official Record of the Debates of the Australasian Federal Convention: 1891–1898*, Melbourne, 3 March 1898, p. 1801 (Henry Higgins).

25 *Immigration Restriction Act 1901* (Cth) section 3(a).

26 Commonwealth, Parliamentary Debates, House of Representatives, 26 September 1901, p. 5233 (Edmund Barton).

27 Nick O'Neill et al., *Retreat from Injustice: Human Rights Law in Australia*, Federation Press, Sydney, 2004, p. 698, citing John Lack and Jacqueline Templeton (eds), *Sources of Australian Immigration History 1901–1945*, University of Melbourne, Melbourne, 1988, pp. 11–12.

28 Commonwealth, Parliamentary Debates, House of Representatives, 24 April 1902, p. 11979 (Isaac Isaacs).

29 ibid., p. 11977 (Henry Higgins).

30 *Commonwealth Franchise Act 1902* (Cth) section 4.

31 Gordon Reid, *That Unhappy Race: Queensland and the Aboriginal Problem, 1838–1901*, Australian Scholarly Publishing, Melbourne, 2006, p. ix.

2 The 1967 referendum

1 Bain Attwood and Andrew Markus, *The 1967 Referendum: Race, Power and the Australian Constitution*, 2nd edition, Aboriginal Studies Press, Canberra, 2007, p. 7.

2 John Gardiner-Garden, *The 1967 Referendum – History and Myths*, Research Brief No. 11, Parliamentary Library, 2006–07, p. 5.

3 AIATSIS, 'We Hereby Make Protest', <aiatsis.gov.au/explore/day-of-mourning>.

4 The Universal Declaration of Human Rights 1948, preamble.

5 John Gardiner-Garden, *The 1967 Referendum – History and Myths*, Research Brief No. 11, Parliamentary Library, 2006–07, p. 72.

6   Commonwealth, Parliamentary Debates, House of Representatives, 9 May 1957, p. 1227 (HV Evatt).

7   Bain Attwood and Andrew Markus, *The 1967 Referendum: Race, Power and the Australian Constitution*, 2nd edition, Aboriginal Studies Press, Canberra, 2007, p. 23.

8   Expert Panel on Constitutional Recognition of Indigenous Australians, *Recognising Aboriginal and Torres Strait Islander Peoples in the Constitution: Report of the Expert Panel*, Report, 16 January 2012, p. 21.

9   Geoffrey Sawer, 'The Australian Constitution and the Australian Aborigine', 1966, *Federal Law Review*, vol. 2, p. 26; Australian Bureau of Statistics, *Aboriginal and Torres Strait Islander Peoples and The Census after the 1967 Referendum*, <https://www.abs.gov.au/ausstats/abs@.nsf/Previousproducts/2071.0Feature%20Article2July%202011?opendocument&tabname=Summary&prodno=2071.0&issue=July%202011&num=&view=>.

10   *The Age*, 22 May 1967, p. 5.

11   ibid.

12   Bain Attwood and Andrew Markus, *The 1967 Referendum: Race, Power and the Australian Constitution*, 2nd edition, Aboriginal Studies Press, Canberra, 2007, pp. 30, 130.

13   ibid., p. 47.

14   Robert French, 'The Race Power: A Constitutional Chimera', in HP Lee and George Winterton (eds), *Australian Constitutional Landmarks*, Cambridge University Press, Melbourne, 2003, p. 190.

15   Geoffrey Sawer, 'The Australian Constitution and the Australian Aborigine', 1967, *Federal Law Review*, vol. 2, p. 35.

16   Bain Attwood and Andrew Markus, *The 1967 Referendum: Race, Power and the Australian Constitution*, 2nd edition, Aboriginal Studies Press, Canberra, 2007, p. 114.

17   George Williams and David Hume, *People Power: The History and Future of the Referendum in Australia*, UNSW Press, Sydney, 2010, p. 149.

18   *Parliamentary Handbook of the Commonwealth of Australia 2011*, 32nd edition, Parliamentary Library, Department of Parliamentary Services, 2011, p. 388.

19   *The Australian*, 29 May 1967, p. 1.

20   ibid.

21   *Sunday Herald*, 28 May 1967, p. 1.

22   Bain Attwood and Andrew Markus, *The 1967 Referendum: Race, Power and the Australian Constitution*, 2nd edition, Aboriginal Studies Press, Canberra, 2007, p. 57.

23   Jackie Huggins, 'The 1967 Referendum … Four Decades Later', Speech delivered for The Sydney Institute, 22 May 2007.

24   Bain Attwood and Andrew Markus, *The 1967 Referendum: Race, Power and the Australian Constitution*, 2nd edition, Aboriginal Studies Press, Canberra, 2007, p. 57.

25   ibid., p. 62.

3   A new era?

1   Jack Horner, *Seeking Racial Justice: An Insider's Memoir of the Movement for Aboriginal Advancement, 1938–1978*, Aboriginal Studies Press, Canberra, 2004, pp. 133–34.

2   ibid., p. 143.

3   Larissa Behrendt, 'Preface', in Gary Foley, Andrew Schaap and Edwina Howell (eds), *The Aboriginal Tent Embassy: Sovereignty, Black Power, Land Rights and the State*, Routledge, London, 2013, p. xxiii.

4   National Museum of Australia, *Campaigning for Land Rights, 1963–68* (Collaborating for Indigenous Rights).

5   Jack Horner, *Seeking Racial Justice: An Insider's Memoir of the Movement for Aboriginal Advancement, 1938–1978*, Aboriginal Studies Press, Canberra, 2004, p. 138.

6   The People of Yirrkala, 'Yolngu Statement in the Gupapunyngu Language', 6 May 1971, <www.kooriweb.org/foley/resources/pdfs/126.pdf>.

7   *Milirrpum v Nabalco Pty Ltd* (1971) 17 *Federal Law Reports* 141, p. 267.

8   The People of Yirrkala, 'Yolngu Statement in the Gupapunyngu Language'.

9   Gary Foley, Andrew Schaap and Edwina Howell (eds), *The Aboriginal Tent Embassy: Sovereignty, Black Power, Land Rights and the State*, Routledge, London, 2013, p. xxv.

10   ibid., p. xxiii.

11   Gough Whitlam, Speech delivered at the Gurindji Land Ceremony, 16 August 1975, <pmtranscripts.pmc.gov.au/release/transcript-3849>.

12   *Coe v Commonwealth* (1979) 24 *Australian Law Reports*, p. 122.

13   LR Hiatt, 'Treaty, Compact, Makarrata …?', *Oceania*, 1987, no. 58, p. 140.

14   Senate Standing Committee on Constitutional and Legal Affairs on the Feasibility of a Compact or 'Makarrata' between the Commonwealth and Aboriginal People, Senate of Australia, *Two Hundred Years Later …*, 1983, p. 115.

15   Australian Constitutional Commission, *Final Report of the Constitutional Commission*, 1988, vol. 1, para. 4.158.

16   ibid., para. 10.372.

17   ibid., para. 10.455.

18   Editorial, 'World Focus on Aborigines', *Sydney Morning Herald*, 19 January 1988.

19   Peter Cochrane and David Goodman, 'The Great Australian Journey: Cultural Logic and Nationalism in the Postmodern Era', *Australian Historical Studies*, 1988, vol. 23, no. 91, p. 25.

20   'Barunga Statement', *Aboriginal Law Bulletin*, 1988, vol. 2, no. 33, p. 16.

21   ibid.

22   Prime Minister Robert Hawke, Speech delivered at the Barunga Sports and Cultural Festival, Northern Territory, 12 June 1988, <pmtranscripts. pmc.gov.au/sites/default/files/original/00007334.pdf>.

23   Murray Goot and Tim Rowse, *Divided Nation?: Indigenous Affairs and the Imagined Public*, Melbourne University Publishing, Melbourne, 2007, p. 77.

24   Murray Goot and Tim Rowse, *Divided Nation?: Indigenous Affairs and the Imagined Public*, Melbourne University Publishing, Melbourne, 2007, p. 77, citing ABC TV, *Four Corners*, 17 March 1986 (Patrick Dodson).

25   'Treaty', Yothu Yindi, Sony/ATV Music Publishing, 1991.

26   *Council for Aboriginal Reconciliation Act 1991* (Cth), preamble.

27   Damien Short, *Reconciliation and Colonial Power: Indigenous Rights in Australia*, Ashgate, Aldershot, 2008, p. 132.

28   Gary Foley, Andrew Schaap and Edwina Howell (eds), *The Aboriginal Tent Embassy: Sovereignty, Black Power, Land Rights and the State*, Routledge, London, 2013, p. 193, citing Margaret Meenaghan, Interview with Kevin Gilbert, 1992.

29   *Council for Aboriginal Reconciliation Act 1991* (Cth), preamble.

30   Prime Minister Paul Keating, 'Opportunity and Care, Dignity and Hope', Speech delivered at Australia's celebration of the 1993 International Year of the World's Indigenous Peoples, Redfern Park, 10 December 1992, <antar. org.au/sites/default/files/paul_keating_speech_transcript.pdf>.

31   *Mabo v Queensland (No. 2)* (1992) 175 *Commonwealth Law Reports*, p. 1.

32   Robert Manne, 'The Howard Years: A Political Interpretation', in Robert Manne (ed.), *The Howard Years*, Black Inc Agenda, Melbourne, 2004, p. 18.

33   Prime Minister John Howard, Speech delivered at the opening ceremony of the Australian Reconciliation Convention, Melbourne, 26 May 1997.

34   Jeremy Cordeaux, Interview with Prime Minister John Howard, 5DN, 5 March 1999, <pmtranscripts.pmc.gov.au/release/transcript-11182>.

35   Commonwealth, Parliamentary Debates, House of Representatives, 26 August 1999, p. 9205 (Prime Minister John Howard).

36   *Kartinyeri v Commonwealth (Hindmarsh Island Bridge Case)*, Transcript of Argument, High Court of Australia, 5 February 1998.

37   Australian Constitutional Convention, *Report of the Constitutional Convention*, Department of Prime Minister and Cabinet, 1998, vol. 3, p. 10.

38   'Recent Documents: Final Resolutions of the Constitutional Convention, Canberra, 2–13 February 1998', *Public Law Review*, 1998, vol. 9, p. 57.

39   Council of Aboriginal Reconciliation, *Going Forward: Social Justice for the First Australians*, AGPS, Canberra, 1995, p. 36.

40   Parliament of Australia, Constitutional Alteration (Preamble) 1999, No. 32 of 1999, 11 August 1999.

41   Helen Lambert, 'A Draft Preamble: Les Murray and the Politics of Poetry', *Journal of Australian Studies*, 2003, vol. 80, no. 27, p. 8, citing Paul Sheehan, 'A Redneck Enjoys the Glow of his Afterlife', *Sydney Morning Herald*, 2 October 1999.

42   Prime Minister John Howard and Senator Aden Ridgeway, Joint Press Conference, 3 November 1999.

43   *Constitutional Alteration (Preamble) Bill 1999* (Cth).

44   ABC Television, 'New Constitution Preamble', *7.30 Report*, 11 August 1999 (Gatjil Djerrkura).

45   ABC Television, 'New Constitution Preamble', *7.30 Report*, 11 August 1999 (Senator Aden Ridgeway).

46   ABC Local Radio, 'Aboriginal Leaders Call for "No" Vote on Preamble', *The World Today*, 3 November 1999 (Peter Yu), <www.abc.net.au/worldtoday/stories/s64063.htm>.

47   Margo Kingston, 'Howard Keen to Reconcile', *Sydney Morning Herald*, 9 November 1999, cited in Mark McKenna, Amelia Simpson and George Williams, 'With Hope in God, the Prime Minister and the Poet: Lessons from the 1999 Referendum on the Preamble', *University of New South Wales Law Journal*, 2001, vol. 24, p. 416.

48   Gatjil Djerrkura, 'Lack of Proper Consultation Sinks Referendum', ATSIC Media Release, 8 November 1999.

49   *Constitution Alteration (Preamble) 1999* (Cth) cl 125A.

50   Mark McKenna, Amelia Simpson and George Williams, 'First Words: The Preamble to the Australian Constitution', *University of New South Wales Law Journal*, 2001, vol. 24, p. 386.

51   Council for Aboriginal Reconciliation, *Reconciliation: Australia's Challenge*, Final Report to the Prime Minister and the Commonwealth Parliament, December 2000, ch. 10.

52   ibid.

53   Sir William Deane, 'Address to Corroboree 2000', Speech delivered on the occasion of Corroboree 2000, Sydney, 27 May 2000, <australianpolitics.com/2000/05/27/governor-general-sir-william-deane-address-to-corroboree-2000.html>.

54   Council for Aboriginal Reconciliation, *The People's Movement*, AustLII, <www5.austlii.edu.au/au/orgs/car/council/spl98_20/goal3.htm>.

55   'Some Marched Alone in Crowd', *Canberra Times*, 3 June 2000, p. 3.

56   John Laws, Interview with John Howard, Prime Minister of Australia, Sydney, 29 May 2000.

57   Debra Jopson, 'Surge in Support for Treaty with Aborigines', *Sydney Morning Herald*, 8 November 2000.

58   Council for Aboriginal Reconciliation, *Reconciliation: Australia's Challenge*, Final Report to the Prime Minister and the Commonwealth Parliament, December 2000, ch. 10.

4   The journey to recognition

1   *Constitution Act 1975* (Vic) section 1A.

2   *Constitution of Queensland 2001* (Qld) preamble; *Constitution Act 1902* (NSW) section 2; *Constitution Act 1934* (SA) section 2.

3   *Constitution Act 1934* (SA) section 2(3).

4   John Howard, 'A New Reconciliation', *The Sydney Papers*, 2007, vol. 19, no. 4, 104 at pp. 108–109.

5   Commonwealth, Parliamentary Debates, House of Representatives, 13 February 2008, p. 167 (Kevin Rudd).

6   ibid., p. 172.

7   Commonwealth, *Australia 2020 Summit: Final Report*, Department of the Prime Minister and Cabinet, 2008, p. 231.

8   *Communiqué from Yolngu and Bininj Leaders at Yirrkala to the Australian Government*, Yolngu and Bininj Leaders' Statement of Intent, 23 July 2008.

9   ibid.
10   Prime Minister Kevin Rudd, 'Joint Press Conference with the Chief
     Minister of the Northern Territory, Paul Henderson', Media Release,
     24 July 2008.
11   Natasha Robinson and Samantha Maiden, 'No Rush to Indigenous
     Amendment to Constitution', *The Australian*, 25 July 2008.
12   Expert Panel on Constitutional Recognition of Indigenous Australians,
     *Recognising Aboriginal and Torres Strait Islander Peoples in the Constitution:
     Report of the Expert Panel*, Report, 16 January 2012, 'Executive Summary',
     p. xi.
13   ibid., p. xviii.
14   *Aboriginal and Torres Strait Islander Peoples Recognition Act 2013* (Cth)
     section 3.
15   Commonwealth, Parliamentary Debates, House of Representatives,
     13 February 2013, p. 1123.
16   ibid.
17   Patricia Karvelas, 'Historic Constitution Vote over Indigenous Recognition
     Facing Hurdles', *The Australian* (online), 20 January 2012, <www.
     theaustralian.com.au/national-affairs/indigenous/historic-constitution-
     vote-over-indigenous-recognition-facing-hurdles/news-story/92c14ff592d
     43981049fdade4280ddbf>.
18   Prime Minister Tony Abbott, 'Australia Day 2014', Media Release and
     Speech, 26 January 2014.
19   Bill Shorten, 'Keynote Address at the Garma Festival', Arnhem, Northern
     Territory, 3 August 2014.
20   Nigel Scullion, 'Next Step Towards Indigenous Constitutional
     Recognition', 28 March 2014, <www.indigenous.gov.au/minister-scullion-
     next-step-towards-indigenous-constitutional-recognition>.
21   Australian National Audit Office, 'Performance Audit Report: Indigenous
     Advancement Strategy', 3 February 2017, <www.anao.gov.au/work/
     performance-audit/indigenous-advancement-strategy>.
22   'Statement Presented by Aboriginal and Torres Strait Islander Attendees
     at a Meeting Held with the Prime Minister and Opposition Leader on
     Constitutional Recognition', 6 July 2015, HC Coombs Centre, Kirribilli,
     Sydney, <www.austlii.edu.au/au/journals/ILB/2015/37.pdf>.

5   The Referendum Council and Uluru process
1   Joint Select Committee on Constitutional Recognition of Aboriginal and
     Torres Strait Islander Peoples, Parliament of Australia, *Interim Report*,
     2014, p. 29.
2   *Commonwealth of Australia Constitution Act 1900* (Imp) 63 & 64 Vict,
     preamble.
3   Indigenous Youth Engagement Council, 'RECOGNISE THIS', Youth
     Report on Constitutional Recognition, National Centre of Indigenous
     Excellence Indigenous Youth Engagement Council, 2013, p. 31.
4   Referendum Council, *Final Report of the Referendum Council*, 2017, p. 11.

5   ibid., p. 10.
6   ibid., p. 2.
7   The Hon. Malcolm Turnbull MP Prime Minister, Senator The Hon.
     George Brandis QC Attorney-General, Senator The Hon. Nigel Scullion
     Minister for Indigenous Affairs, 'Joint Press Release: Response to
     Referendum Council's report on Constitutional Reform', 26 October 2017,
     <www.malcolmturnbull.com.au/media/response-to-referendum-councils-
     report-on-constitutional-recognition>.
8   Parliament of the Commonwealth of Australia, Joint Select Committee
     on Constitutional Recognition relating to Aboriginal and Torres Strait
     Islander Peoples, *Final Report* (November 2018), Recommendation 1,
     p. xvii.
9   Ken Wyatt, 'A Voice for Indigenous Australians', Media Release,
     30 October 2019.
10   Ken Wyatt, 'National Press Club Address – Walking in Partnership to
     Effect Change', Speech, 10 July 2019.
11   Ken Wyatt, 'Voice Co-Design Underway', Media Release, 13 November
     2019.
12   National Indigenous Australians Agency, *Indigenous Voice Co-design
     Process: Final Report to the Australian Government*, 2021, p. 9.
13   ibid., p. 7.
14   ibid., p. 10.
15   ibid., p. 11.
16   ibid., p. 12.

6   Voice, Treaty, Truth
1   Anne Twomey, 'Why an Indigenous Voice Would Not Be a "Third
     Chamber" of Parliament', *Sydney Morning Herald*, 28 May 2019, <www.
     smh.com.au/national/why-an-indigenous-voice-would-not-be-third-
     chamber-of-parliament-20190526-p51r7t.html>.
2   Referendum Council, *Final Report of the Referendum Council*, 30 June 2017,
     <www.referendumcouncil.org.au/sites/default/files/report_attachments/
     Referendum_Council_Final_Report.pdf>, p. 2.
3   Murray Gleeson, 'Recognition in Keeping with the Constitution:
     A Worthwhile Project' (2019), p. 12.
4   Referendum Council, *Final Report of the Referendum Council*, 30 June 2017,
     <www.referendumcouncil.org.au/sites/default/files/report_attachments/
     Referendum_Council_Final_Report.pdf>, pp. 30–31.
5   ibid., p. 14.
6   ibid.
7   ibid., p. 18.

7   The Voice
1   'Read Incoming Prime Minister Anthony Albanese's Full Speech After
     Labor Wins Federal Election', ABC News, 22 May 2022, <www.abc.
     net.au/news/2022-05-22/anthony-albanese-acceptance-speech-full-
     transcript/101088736>.

2   Anthony Albanese, 'Address to Garma Festival', Speech, 30 July 2022, <www.pm.gov.au/media/address-garma-festival>.

3   Aboriginal and Torres Strait Islander Voice, 'Referendum Working Group Terms of Reference', Guideline, 28 September 2022, <voice.gov.au/resources/referendum-working-group-terms-reference>.

4   Aboriginal and Torres Strait Islander Voice, 'Voice Principles', Guideline, 3 April 2023, <voice.gov.au/about-voice/voice-principles>.

5   *Advice of the Referendum Working Group to the Government on the Constitutional Amendment and Referendum Question*, 23 March 2023, <voice.gov.au/news/advice-referendum-working-group-government-constitutional-amendment-and-referendum-question>.

6   *House of Representatives Hansard*, 30 March 2023, p. 1.

7   Joint Select Committee on the Aboriginal and Torres Strait Islander Voice Referendum, *Advisory Report on the Constitution Alteration (Aboriginal and Torres Strait Islander Voice) 2023*, Report, May 2023, p. xi.

8   *Communiqué for the Referendum Working Group*, Media Release, 2 February 2023, <ministers.pmc.gov.au/burney/2023/communique-referendum-working-group>.

9   This text includes an extract from the International Court of Justice in its Advisory Opinion on Western Sahara (1975) International Court of Justice Reports, pp. 85–86, quoted in *Mabo v Queensland (No. 2)* (1992) 175 *Commonwealth Law Reports*, p. 41.

10   Anne Twomey, 'Why an Indigenous Voice Would Not Be a "Third Chamber" of Parliament', *Sydney Morning Herald*, 28 May 2019, <www.smh.com.au/national/why-an-indigenous-voice-would-not-be-third-chamber-of-parliament-20190526-p51r7t.html>.

11   *Canada Act 1982* (UK) c 11, schedule B, section 35(1).

12   *Constitution of the Kingdom of Norway* (1814) article 108. Prior to amendments to the Norwegian Constitution in 2014, this provision was located in section 110a.

13   *Constitution of Finland* (1999) section 17.

14   Attorney-General Mark Dreyfus, Submission No 64 to Joint Select Committee on the Aboriginal and Torres Strait Islander Voice Referendum, Parliament of Australia, *Inquiry into the Aboriginal and Torres Strait Islander Voice Referendum*, 21 April 2023.

8   The Voice referendum

1   Commonwealth, Parliamentary Debates, House of Representatives, 16 December 1912, p. 7154 (William Hughes).

2   Commonwealth, Parliamentary Debates, House of Representatives, 16 December 1912, p. 7156 (Andrew Fisher).

3   Commonwealth of Australia, *Official Pamphlet for the Referendums to be Held on Saturday, the 31st Day of May, 1913* (1913).

4   Commonwealth of Australia, *Budget Measures: Budget Paper No 2*, 9 May 2023, p. 85.

INDEX

INDEX